GOD SAID YES!

Why God Never Rejects, Only Redirects

By
Gaytan Glover Sr, PhD

G3Publishing

ISBN 979-8-9939173-0-6 Hardcover
ISBN 979-8-9939173-1-3 Soft Cover
ISBN 979-8-9939173-2-0 Digital

URL found in the back of this book to obtain the Free Study Guide.

Cover design by Petra Pechova, image generated with AI assistance
Interior formatting by Sonia Martínez

This book was published with the assistance of Goodwill Media Services, Cary, NC. We help publish transformative books for leaders and lay people across America. To publish your book, go to **goodwillmediaservices.com** for more information, or contact us at **goodwillmediaservices@gmail.com**

Printed in the United States of America Contents

ACKNOWLEDGMENTS

To my Lord and Savior Jesus Christ, who said "Yes" to me before I even knew to ask.

To my beloved wife, Jacquetta, whose story of faith and perseverance demonstrates God's faithfulness in the most profound ways. You are a living testament to God's "Yes."

To our children, who teach us daily about trust, faith, and the beauty of God's perfect timing.

To the congregations we've been privileged to serve, especially in Germany and Hawaii, your faith has strengthened ours.

To Dr. Paul Ruffin for your friendship, mentorship, and the powerful foreword that sets the stage for this message.

To every person who prayed for us, encouraged us, and believed in the message of this book.

And to you, the reader, who has journeyed with us through these pages. May you discover the fullness of God's "Yes" in your own life.

TABLE OF CONTENTS

FOREWORD

More than 15 years ago, while Dr. Gaytan G. Glover, Sr. was serving as the State President of the Young Men of Valor Group, I had the grand opportunity to work with him in designing workshops to prepare young men for their roles in society and their spiritual journey. The primary objective of the workshops was to equip the young men of the church with the tools to become confident, well-rounded, skillful leaders.

Dr. Glover, who is a construction engineer, served in the military as supervisor of a combat operations section while deployed in Iraq. He has served as a pastor and taught Church Growth Seminars in Bible College and Theological Seminary. Dr. Glover is an amazing teacher and a dynamic speaker. The writing of this book represents a pivotal moment in his lifelong commitment to making a difference.

In a world where countless believers wrestle with the silence of unanswered prayers and the sting of seemingly divine rejections, Dr. Glover's book, *God Said Yes*, offers a revolutionary perspective that challenges the very foundation of how we understand God's communication with His children. What if everything you've been taught about God's responses to prayer, the traditional "Yes," "No," or "Wait," is fundamentally incomplete? I believe that after reading *God Said Yes*, you will be convinced that the God who declares in His Word that all His promises are "Yes" and in Him "Amen," never says "No" when we ask according to His will.

God Said Yes isn't merely an abstract theological discussion. It transforms how you approach your Monday morning commute, navigate career transitions, face health crises, and guide your children through life's disappointments. Whether you're a new believer grappling with prayers that seem to bounce off the ceiling, a seasoned church member experiencing spiritual burnout, or someone walking through a season of doubt, *God Said Yes* offers a lens that will revolutionize how you see God's hand in every circumstance.

Dr. Glover shares personal testimonies, biblical narratives, and theological exploration in his book, *God Said Yes*. You will discover how God speaks, whether through direct answers, circumstantial guidance, or scriptural wisdom, always working toward your ultimate good and His glory. *God Said Yes* isn't prosperity theology or «name it and claim it» thinking. It is a deep dive into understanding God's nature as fundamentally affirmative, even when His responses require our growth, patience, or redirection.

God Said Yes examines the character of God Himself, His existence, personality, nature, grace, and sovereignty, before exploring how biblical figures like Moses, David, and Jesus exemplify divine guidance rather than divine rejection. You will learn to distinguish between God's instructions, redirections, and His perfect timing. *God Said Yes* provides the fundamentals for you to understand that what we often interpret as «No» is actually God's loving guidance toward something better.

From David's desire to build the temple (his vision was redirected to Solomon) to Moses' consequences for disobedience (lessons learned in following divine instructions), each chapter builds a compelling case that God's fundamental nature is to affirm, guide, and bless, never to reject those who seek Him with pure hearts. *God Said Yes* will challenge you to examine your motives, align your requests with God's will, and trust that when you seek His kingdom first, His «Yes» becomes the foundation for a transformed life. The principles you'll discover aren't theoretical, they are practical, life-changing truths that have guided Dr. Glover through military service, law enforcement, pastoral ministry, and the journey to finding his God-ordained wife. Thank you, Dr. Glover, for writing such a needed book that every Christian can realize a benefit.

As you embark on this exploration, prepare to see prayer, faith, and God's guidance in an entirely new light. Prepare to discover that the God who loves you has been saying "Yes" all along, you just need to learn His language.

Paul Ruffin, Ph.D., D. Min.
Pastor, Professor, & Chief Scientist

Lord, as we move forward in the discovery or reminder of Your perfect will for our lives, we ask that You keep our heart and mind open to receive what You have for us in Your Word, Amen.

ENDORSEMENT

"God Said Yes!" is more than a book—it's a theological breakthrough. Dr. Glover confronts centuries of religious assumptions and reframes how believers interpret God's responses to prayer. His insight that divine delay is not divine denial is both revolutionary and restorative. Every chapter blends biblical scholarship, practical faith, and human experience into a powerful reminder that God's nature is always affirming, never rejecting. This work belongs in seminaries, sanctuaries, and every believer's home who's ever asked, 'Why not me, Lord?' Read it—and you'll never pray the same way again.

Dr Robert J. Watkin

PREFACE

In a world where disappointment often masquerades as divine rejection, where it seems our prayers are unanswered, leave believers questioning God's goodness, and where the phrase "God said no" has become an accepted explanation for life's setbacks, this book dares to challenge a fundamental assumption about how our Heavenly Father responds to His children.

What if everything you've been taught about prayer, specifically about God's responses, has been incomplete? What if the traditional framework of "Yes," "No," or "Wait" doesn't fully capture the heart of a God whose very nature is love, whose promises are sure, and whose will for His children is always good?

This exploration began not in a seminary classroom or during pastoral preparation, but in the trenches of real life, through twenty-four years of military service, decades of ministry across three continents, and the countless moments when I found myself wrestling with what appeared to be God's silence or rejection. As a Military Police Investigator, I learned that evidence often reveals truths that initial assumptions obscure. As a pastor who has shepherded congregations from Hawaii to Iowa to Alabama, I've witnessed firsthand the spiritual damage that occurs when believers misunderstand God's character and responses.

The pages that follow represent more than theological theory; they constitute a paradigm shift that can revolutionize your prayer life, restore your confidence in God's goodness, and realign your understanding of divine communication. Through careful examination of Scripture, personal testimony, and practical application, we will discover that God's fundamental response to prayers offered according to His will is not conditional, it's consistently affirmative.

This book doesn't just contribute to abstract discussions about faith and prayer, it provides practical insights that can transform your daily life. Imagine approaching your job search with the confidence that God's "yes" is already in motion or facing a health crisis with the assurance that God's affirmative response is unfolding in ways you might not yet see. For parents, this perspective can reshape how you guide your children through disappointments. For professionals, it can influence decision-making in ethical dilemmas.

Whether you're a new believer grappling with unanswered prayers, a long-time saint facing spiritual burnout, or someone in a season of doubt, this book offers a fresh lens through which to view life's challenges and opportunities. By understanding God's "yes," you can find new strength for your Monday morning commute, renewed purpose in your relationships, and a revitalized approach to your spiritual disciplines.

The journey we'll take together moves from establishing God's affirming nature to understanding His character, from examining biblical examples to exploring practical applications. We'll walk with Moses, David, and Daniel's friends, learning how their experiences reveal God's consistent pattern of guidance, redirection, and provision rather than rejection. Most importantly, we'll discover how to align our hearts with God's will so that His "yes" becomes the soundtrack of our spiritual lives.

My prayer is that as you turn these pages, the Holy Spirit will illuminate truths that have perhaps been obscured by tradition or misunderstanding. May you discover not just theological concepts, but life-changing realities that draw you closer to the heart of a Father who delights in saying "yes" to His children.

The evidence is compelling. The testimonies are powerful. The scriptural foundation is solid. All that remains is for you to open your heart and mind to a truth that might just transform everything you thought you knew about prayer, faith, and the character of Almighty God.

Gaytan G. Glover Sr.

INTRODUCTION

This book is a comprehensive exploration of the concept of God's responses to our requests, specifically focusing on the fact that God's answer to our requests, according to His will, are always a "Yes." This book doesn't just contribute to abstract discussions about faith and prayer, it provides practical insights that can transform your daily life. Imagine approaching your job search with the confidence that God's "yes" is already in motion or facing a health crisis with the assurance that God's affirmative response is unfolding in ways you might not yet see. For parents, this perspective can reshape how you guide your children through disappointments. For professionals, it can influence decision-making in ethical dilemmas. Whether you're a new believer grappling with unanswered prayers, a long-time ecclesiastical thoroughbred facing burnout, or someone in a season of doubt, this book offers a fresh lens in your view of life's challenges and opportunities. By understanding God's "yes," you can find new strength for your Monday morning commute, renewed purpose in your relationships, and a revitalized approach to your spiritual disciplines.

This book explores personal anecdotes, biblical narratives, and theological reflections to reveal how God communicates with us, whether through direct answers, guidance through circumstances, or the teachings of Scripture, always aiming toward the ultimate good and growth of the individual.

We will tackle several themes central to Christian theology and personal spirituality, such as the nature and personality of God, the importance of seeking God's kingdom and righteousness, God's grace, and the significance of building a personal relationship with Jesus Christ. It emphasizes the belief in God who is actively involved in the lives of believers, guiding, teaching, and sometimes disciplining us to bring about the best in us.

Through the examples of biblical figures like Moses, David, and through Jesus' teachings and actions, you will see how God's responses are not negative or merely immediate but are instead aligned with a larger, often incomprehensible divine plan. The narrative encourages believers to trust in God's wisdom, to seek His will in all things, and to remain faithful even when the path is unclear. It also touches upon the human tendency to desire immediate answers or to misunderstand God's intentions, highlighting the importance of patience, faith, and open-hearted seeking in the spiritual journey. The notion that God answers "No" when we ask according to His will is not a comforting idea, and it's a challenging idea for believers to grapple with because nowhere in the Bible does God say "No" when you ask and He gets the glory and not you yourselves.

This book can serve as a meaningful contribution to discussions about faith, prayer, and the understanding of God's will. It encourages a deep and nuanced engagement with one's spirituality and offers insights that could be valuable to individuals at various stages of their faith journey. Whether for personal reflection or group study, this work prompts you to consider the complexities of divine-human communication and to find peace in the trust that God's answers, whatever form they may take, are ultimately for your good.

CHAPTER ONE

God Is, The Yes God

This foundational chapter challenges the traditional understanding that God responds to prayer with "Yes," "No," or "Wait." Through personal anecdotes and biblical analysis, I argue that God's fundamental nature is affirmative, and what we interpret as "No" answers are actually guidance, redirection, or preparation.

The chapter explores the definition of "No" and examines 2 Corinthians 1:18–20, which declares that all God's promises are "Yes" and "Amen." Using examples of parental guidance, I illustrate how loving authority figures provide reasons and conditions rather than flat rejections, suggesting God operates similarly with His children.

This book seeks to address a controversial question that has puzzled believers for generations: "Does God say no?" Traditionally, believers have understood God's answers to prayer as falling into three categories: "Yes," "No," or "Wait." This simplistic view, while comforting to some, may not fully capture the complexity of God's communication with us.

The Definition of "No"

Webster's dictionary defines "No" as "a negative used to express dissent, denial, or refusal, as in response to a question or request." But does this definition align with God's character and His interactions with His people?

There was a time when I was much younger, I asked my mother if I could go outside to play. She replied, "You haven't cleaned up the house yet." This wasn't a direct "No," but rather a condition that needed to be met before the request could be granted. Saturday morning was cleanup time in the Glover house. If you didn't do it on Friday evening, Saturday morning it was cleanup time. I must say, television watches better in a clean house.

She didn't say maybe or wait. Joyce Marie Glover just replied with the reason why I was not going outside. Now, I could have gone outside anyway, used the excuse that she did not say no, and suffered consequences for my actions, or finished cleaning up the house and asked again, with her blessing. I did the latter. I finished my chores and asked again. She saw that it was clean and said yes. She never said no. If she had said no, that would have meant, "don't ask me again." Still cloudy on this? Let me give another example.

Arbie, my father, would be setting me up for failure if, at twelve years old, I asked for the keys to the car and Daddy gave me the keys to his car and said, "Be safe." I, being only twelve years old, would be too young to drive or even understand the operation of the vehicle and the laws governing the road. Daddy would know that I was not ready.

What does he do? He did not say no; he told me that I was not ready to drive. Daddy took me out and taught me how to drive. When I was sixteen, I got a few years older, practiced, and passed the driving test. After I passed the driving test, I was able to drive. Five years later I asked, "Dad, can I use the car to go to the movie?" He said yes. Again, there was not a no; there was preparation on my part.

I do understand that when the children of Israel, or Moses, or David, and any other person in the Bible asked God for something, God would answer in a way that we understand to be a no. I also understand that when we follow the will of God for our lives, we fall under the rule, "If you seek His face and His righteousness rule, everything else will be added to you" (Matthew 6:33).

It is getting to that point of truth and believing it that is a challenge for believers. In the Bible, I can find where God answers "Yes." However, I cannot see where God gave a flat-out "No" answer, or even a "No; I will not," or how about, "No, you can't do that," or "No, do it yourself," or "No, you got in it, you get out of it!" Well, you can't find one.

We'll even see where, when God says He will do something for you or reveals a plan to you, you can believe that He will make good on what He says He will do.

Biblical Perspective on God's Answers

In the Gospel of Matthew, 6th chapter, you will read that God already knows what we need, and if we seek first the kingdom of God and all His righteousness, that everything else will be added to us. What I was not clear about was when I was told God says no.

> Webster's definition: **No:** *a negative used to express dissent, denial, or refusal, as in response to a question or request. Also used to emphasize or introduce a negative statement.*

There are other expressions you may have heard before or even used, such as the "no's" and "not now's," the "waits," and the "maybe, maybe not" of God. The truth is that "no" is not the person of God.

> *"But as God is true, our word toward you was not yea and nay. For the Son of God, Jesus Christ, who was preached among you by us, even by me and Silvanus and Timotheus, was not yea and nay, but in him was yea. For all the promises of God in him are yea, and in him Amen, unto the glory of God by us"* (2 Corinthians 1:18–20, KJV).

You may want to read verse twenty again and really get what the words say: "all of the promises..." and "...unto the glory of God..." God's promises are "Yes" and "Amen." This passage emphasizes that all of God's promises are affirmative. It states, "For all the promises of God in Him are Yes, and in Him Amen, to the glory of God through us" (NKJV). We want to make sure that when we finish with this evidence, we know that when we are living life to the glory of God, the answer will be yes!

We can certainly list the times our parents, grandparents, uncles, aunts (or TT's), and other "grown folks" in our lives have said, "No." When I read the Bible and see that everywhere there is a negative answer, it is combined with the reason why whatever was asked got a response that sounded like God said No. Now, I am not crazy, I understand what a no is. I wanted to understand why there was not a flat-out, "No, you can't have that!" "No, you can't, no, no, no!" Instead, what we often interpret as a "No" is actually God providing guidance, redirection, or preparation.

The lack of explicit "No" answers in the Bible is instead filled with numerous instances of God answering "Yes."

If we take a moment to reminisce back through our lives, notice the times when we gave an answer of no, and because the person kept asking, we said yes. After we changed our answer to yes, that person continued asking for something else and eventually learned how to manipulate you to get a yes answer. In some cases, the person got confused by the sometimes yes and sometimes no answers to the same questions.

You can't manipulate God. His answer will always be yes.

Wait, before you think, "You've got to be kidding me, God said no to me yesterday." Why do I say that, when all you seem to get is a no from God when you ask God, for instance, to keep your sick mother alive, or "Lord I want a baby, please, can I have one?" or the famous request, "Lord, can I have a million dollars?"

The interplay between God's sovereignty and human free will is a profound theological concept that deserves deeper consideration. If God were to issue absolute, immutable "No" responses, it could potentially negate our free will, a gift that God Himself bestowed upon us.

This presents us with a theological conundrum: how does an all-powerful, all-knowing God interact with His creation without overriding their ability to make choices? The resolution lies in understanding God's nature as revealed in Scripture.

In Jeremiah 29:11 (NIV), God says, "*For I know the plans I have for you, plans to prosper you and not to harm you, plans to give you hope and a future.*" This verse suggests that God's intentions for us are always positive, aligning with our earlier assertion that God's responses are fundamentally affirmative.

However, this doesn't mean God simply acquiesces to our every desire. Rather, His "Yes" often comes in the form of guidance, redirection, or even loving discipline. As the writer of Hebrews states, *"No discipline seems pleasant at the time, but painful. Later, however, it produces a harvest of righteousness and peace for those who have been trained by it"* (Hebrews 12:11, NIV).

This understanding allows us to reconcile God's sovereignty with our free will. God, in His infinite wisdom, provides direction and sets boundaries but ultimately allows us to make choices. His "Yes" might sometimes look like a "No" to our limited human perspective, but it's always in service of His greater "Yes" to our ultimate good and His glory.

Consider the apostle Paul's experience with his *"thorn in the flesh"* (2 Corinthians 12:7-9, NIV). Paul pleaded with God three times to remove it, but God's response was, *"My grace is sufficient for you, for my power is made perfect in weakness."* This wasn't a "No," but a "Yes" to a greater purpose that Paul couldn't initially see.

This deeper understanding of God's responses challenges us to trust in His wisdom even when we don't understand, to seek His will rather than merely His approval of our plans, and to view His guidance, even when it seems negative, as an affirmation of His love and His perfect plan for our lives.

Be glad that when you seek God's counsel, you get good counsel every time. Are you willing to ask for counsel? I had to realize that every time I have consulted God for a matter, not asking Him, but consulting with Him in every matter, He is faithful and just to give me good counsel.

Don't get me wrong, sometimes I didn't get it right, meaning I didn't seek Him first because, to tell the truth, I knew what the answer would be but did it my way with my understanding. There were times that I needed to stop doing something or go to places I should not have gone but went anyway. It was I who made the choice to listen to the ungodly advice of other counsel, usually because the other counsel was more of what I wanted to hear and not so much of what I needed to hear and do at that time.

I can remember a time when I was trying to get my walk right. I was at the crossroads of living a saved life and walking on the edge of a worldly track to nowhere.

I was in California, and it was a Friday night. Greater Victory Temple COGIC, Seaside, had services on Friday as well as Sunday. Some of the seasoned leaders suggested that I go on Fridays if I wanted a breakthrough in my life. If I wanted to get right, I knew I needed to be there.

I can remember a friend of mine who occasionally attended church with me informing me that a new club had opened in downtown Monterey and that we should go. Now, I knew I was not supposed to be leaving the church to go to a club. This 20-year-old (me) sure did. We snuck out of service to go to this club.

If you are saying, "Why did you sneak out of the church? You were a grown man; you could have walked out," wrong will have you sneaking around like a teenage child. It will do that to you.

I felt so guilty leaving, but I put my finger up (in some cultures when you get up during service to go to the bathroom, you put your index finger up in the air as if to visually motion to wait one moment as you leave the room, or it could also mean excuse me). I can't make that up. You ask someone from the "olden days."

Anyway, we left and went to the club. There was a line so long we stood outside for a good ten minutes before this lady evangelist came up behind me and yelled, "Are you saved?" I didn't know who she was, but I answered, "Yes!"

Immediately, conviction ran through me. I had left the church to go to a club, and you know nothing good for the soul can be found at a club. I knew that but did it anyway. I believe God sent someone to check my soul. Did I really believe what I professed?

I could have said "Leave me alone, crazy lady" or "No." After I said yes, I told my buddy, "Let's go," and we left.

I believe that this account in the Bible can address good or bad counsel better than me. Let's look at a scripture to help understand the seeking of godly counsel, because God speaks through His Word and others whom He has given the learned tongue and the ear, as the scripture confirms in Isaiah 50:4. Let me put my finger up and get to the Word.

The Story of Rehoboam: Seeking Godly Counsel

In 1 Kings 12, we find a powerful example of seeking godly counsel. After Solomon's death, Rehoboam faced a crucial decision: would he lighten the burden on the people as they requested? He first consulted with the elders who had served his father, and they advised him to serve the people with kindness. Instead, Rehoboam rejected their wisdom and turned to his young friends, who told him to increase the people's burden.

The young men told him to say, *"My little finger shall be thicker than my father's loins. And now whereas my father did lade you with a heavy yoke, I will add to your yoke: my father hath chastised you with whips, but I will chastise you with scorpions"* (1 Kings 12:11, KJV).

When they came to Rehoboam on the third day, he gave them the answer his friends suggested. He did not take the advice of the old men. He ordered more to their yoke and reminded them that his father also corrected them with whips, but that he would correct with scorpions, which was a whip with sharp bones or metal chips tied at the end.

The result? The kingdom divided, and Rehoboam's advisor Adoram was stoned to death when he tried to enforce the harsh decree. The king barely escaped with his life.

This narrative emphasizes the critical importance of seeking God's counsel. The background is significant: God had already told the prophet Ahijah that He would tear the kingdom from Solomon's hand due to Israel's idolatry.

In chapters 10 and 11, God sent Ahijah the Shilonite to Jeroboam with a message. Ahijah met Jeroboam on his journey while wearing a new robe. Ahijah tore his robe into twelve pieces. He told Jeroboam, "*Take ten pieces for yourself, for this is what the Lord, the God of Israel, says: 'See, I am going to tear the kingdom out of Solomon's hand and give you ten tribes. But for the sake of my servant David and the city of*

Jerusalem, which I have chosen out of all the tribes of Israel, he will have one tribe'" (NIV).

He did this because they had turned away from God to worship the pagan goddess Ashtoreth, the pagan gods Chemosh and Molek, and they walked in disobedience and did nothing right in God's sight. They didn't even keep His decrees and laws as David did.

If we seek God's kingdom and His righteousness first, the right decisions can be made. If we choose to go against God and do our own thing, all of that will be added too. It goes both ways. If you don't seek His counsel first, the decision and the consequence will be added to you also.

Let me give you a real-life example. If you don't ask for God's counsel before making decisions (maybe you know the right decision to make but do the opposite) and that decision places you in debt or something similar, don't go asking God, "Why me, why me Lord?" Ask yourself if you had consulted God first. If the answer to that question is no, you did not ask God, repent.

And if it took you nine months to get into this debt or mess, it may take you nine months to get out of that situation. I am not going to tell you that God won't or can't bring you out immediately because He did it for Peter in the book of Matthew when he walked on the water. He has also done it for me on many occasions.

I just know that we tend to ask God to be a genie in a bottle. Whenever we mess up, we expect Him to deliver a "right now" cleanup. Don't be surprised if God teaches you how to budget for another nine months, or to refrain from that "thing," remain pure for a time, or whatever it is that you find yourself in.

If He says no, would you have free will to choose? If God says no, it will never happen, whatever it is will never happen. As you will see in the few examples that follow, God will listen and hear everything you ask Him. He is the Counselor.

God as a Counselor, rather than simply saying "No," God often provides reasons, guidance, or alternative paths. This approach preserves our free will while offering divine wisdom. God's ability to exceed our expectations, Ephesians 3:20 (KJV), reminds us that God *"is able to do exceedingly abundantly above all that we ask or think."* This suggests that God's responses will always go beyond our limited understanding or expectations.

Addressing Common Objections

As we explore this perspective on God's responses, it's important to address some common objections that may arise:

"But I've prayed for something, and it didn't happen. Isn't that a 'No'?"

This is perhaps the most common objection to the idea that God always says "Yes." However, we must remember that God's perspective is eternal and all-knowing, while ours is limited and temporal. What may seem like a "No" to us could be God's "Yes" to something better or more aligned with His will.

Consider the story of Paul's thorn in the flesh (2 Corinthians 12:7-9, KJV). Paul prayed three times for God to remove it, but God's response was, *"My grace is sufficient for you, for my power is made perfect in weakness."* This wasn't a "No," but a "Yes" to a greater purpose that Paul couldn't initially see.

I have a thorn in my side. I often stutter, and I have a learning disability. Yes, I wrote it. For years, I have battled with dyslexia. Dyslexia is a learning disability that affects my reading and spelling the most. I have always been a person that can articulate complex things in a simplistic way when I write. I like to write because I can express myself without stuttering.

When I was 15, I had to speak at Second Baptist Church in Olathe, Kansas. That was the first time I had spoken publicly, and I loved it! I knew at that point that preaching was my calling. My mother even told me after that I should "put your money where your mouth is," meaning invest in my talent. I really wanted to, but there was one thing, I could not read well, and it scared me to read openly, not because of the crowd but because of the disability.

I remember when I was in California, I asked God to "please, Lord, fix my tongue and my decoding of words when I speak." You know what the Lord told me? "Read."

"What? Read, Lord?" That's what you have for me? "I've been reading," I protested. He said, "Read my Word."

Just in case you're wondering, He didn't crack the ceiling open with a big loud voice that shook the room, no, that didn't happen. He just told me to read. I picked up a thesaurus and started from beginning to end.

What about the Word? No, I did not start with the Bible because back then we didn't have all the versions and translations available now. It took me another three years before I actually did what the Lord told me to do. I was afraid of the

Bible because I could not pronounce those big Bible words. You may know some: thou, thus, and shall. To a guy who stutters, those are big words.

I was in Germany when I finally accepted my calling to the ministry and started reading the Word. As I read the Bible, I not only started reading better, but I understood the Word. Did all this mean that I was not intelligent, not smart, or like the kids called me in school, dumb? No, it meant that I had to learn differently.

I have added a portion in the study guide to assist those with my "unique" learning ability.

God did not tell Paul no, but God's grace was sufficient. Moses stuttered, and God had Aaron on his side. Then there is me. I still have a unique learning ability. Does that stop me? No. Did God tell me no, He would not heal my tongue? No, He did not. His grace and guidance are sufficient for me.

As a result, even though I did not have faith in the education system, I went back to school because I felt that being one of the 8%ers would give me confidence. Yes, I am in the 8% of African Americans in the U.S. who have earned a doctorate, but I am still overcoming the unique ability daily.

"Doesn't the Bible show instances where God said 'No'?"

While there are instances in the Bible that may appear as God saying "No," upon closer examination, these are often cases of God providing guidance, redirection, or preparation.

For example, when David wanted to build the temple, God redirected this task to Solomon (1 Chronicles 28:2–3, ESV). This wasn't a "No" to honoring God, but a "Yes" to a different plan that involved both David and Solomon.

When God judges, He is saying "Yes" to His own righteous nature and "Yes" to the protection and vindication of His people. As Psalm 9:8 (NIV) states, "He rules the world in righteousness and judges the people with equity."

By addressing these objections, we deepen our understanding of God's "Yes." We see that it's not a simplistic affirmation of our every whim, but a complex, loving response that always aligns with His perfect will and our ultimate good.

Free Will and God's Responses

Did God say "no" to Israel regarding the Promised Land? Did Moses ask to go into the Promised Land? No. God appointed him to go get the children of Israel from Egypt and take them to a Promised Land. They didn't need to ask God to take them to the land. God had a plan for them.

The plan for the ones who originally left Egypt changed when they plotted to stone Moses and his followers. God visited the children in the tabernacle after they threatened Moses. God said to Moses, *"How long will they provoke me? and how long before they believe me, for all the signs which I have showed among them?"* (Numbers 14:11, KJV)

For them, it was because of the "but" that changed whether they would get to the Promised Land. In the book of Numbers, the fourteenth chapter and the tenth verse, we learn that all the congregation decided, "Let's stone them" (Moses and Caleb). It was at that time God took the Promised Land away from the children of Israel except Caleb. They disqualified themselves when they rebelled against God.

Reacting with knowledge of God's character, to truly understand God's responses, we must study His character through Scripture. This knowledge helps us interpret His guidance correctly and align our lives with His will.

It's okay to react to information that we receive, but when we start rebelling against God, that reaction will get us into trouble. That disqualifies us from His blessings, the answers, the healings, etc.

The relationship between God's guidance and human choice, if God were to give absolute "No" answers, it might infringe upon our free will. Instead, God's guidance allows us to make choices while providing wisdom and direction.

The importance of knowing God through His Word, as we continue to explore and understand the character and person of God through His Word, we'll find that His fundamental nature is to affirm and guide, not to negate. Let's strive to know God more deeply, trusting in His wisdom and guidance in all aspects of our lives.

Self-Evaluation Questions:

- **Personal Reflection:** I shared examples from my childhood where my parents set conditions rather than giving a flat «No.» Think about your own experiences with authority figures. Can you identify times when what seemed like a «No» was actually guidance or preparation for something better?
- **Biblical Analysis:** Examine 2 Corinthians 1:18–20, which states that *"all the promises of God in Him are Yes, and in Him Amen."* How does this verse challenge traditional

views about God's responses to prayer? What implications does this have for how we understand God's character?

- **Free Will Consideration:** I argued that if God gave absolute «No» responses, it could potentially negate our free will. Do you agree or disagree with this perspective? How do you reconcile God's sovereignty with human freedom to choose?
- **Prayer and Counsel:** Reflecting on the story about leaving church to go to a club, discuss how seeking godly counsel differs from simply doing what we want. How can we better distinguish between God's voice and our own desires when making decisions?
- **Scripture Investigation:** I mention that I couldn't find explicit «No» answers from God in the Bible, but rather explanations and guidance. Choose a biblical story where it might appear God said «No» and analyze whether it was actually redirection, preparation, or something else entirely.

Moment of Prayer:

Lord, as I look upon Your magnificent creation, the vastness of the skies, the intricate design of a flower, the rhythm of the seasons, I see Your eternal power and divine nature clearly displayed. Thank You that every sunrise declares Your faithfulness, every star proclaims Your majesty, and every breath I take testifies to Your sustaining love. Help me to see You not just as a distant God, but as the intimate Creator who formed me with purpose and continues to shape my daily walk with You. Amen!

CHAPTER TWO

Getting to Know God

Before understanding God's responses, you must first know God's character. This chapter systematically explores five key aspects of God's nature: His existence (established through creation and requiring faith), His personality (showing Him as relational and responsive), His fundamental nature (love, light, consuming fire, and spirit), His grace (unmerited favor that saves and transforms), and His sovereignty (demonstrated through God's response to Job, highlighting His supreme authority over all creation). Each aspect is supported by Scripture and practical application, building a comprehensive foundation for understanding how God interacts with His people.

The Existence of God

We begin our journey of understanding God by acknowledging His existence. The Bible opens with a profound statement in Genesis 1:1–2 (KJV):

> *"In the beginning God created the heavens and the earth. And the earth was without form, and void; and dark-*

ness was upon the face of the deep. And the Spirit of God moved upon the face of the waters."

This passage not only asserts God's existence but also His role as Creator. The apostle Paul further emphasizes this in Romans 1:20 (KJV):

"For the invisible things of him from the creation of the world are clearly seen, being understood by the things that are made, even his eternal power and Godhead; so that they are without excuse."

As we recognize God's existence, we're called to have faith in Him. Hebrews 11:5–6 (KJV) underscores this:

"By faith Enoch was translated that he should not see death; and was not found, because God had translated him: for before his translation he had this testimony, that he pleased God. But without faith it is impossible to please him: for he that cometh to God must believe that he is, and that he is a rewarder of them that diligently seek him."

The Personality of God

Having established God's existence, we can explore His personality. God is not an impersonal force, but a living, personal being. 1 Thessalonians 1:9 (KJV) describes Him as "the living and true God."

God's personality is multifaceted, encompassing a range of emotions and attitudes:

- **God loves:** *"He that loveth not knoweth not God; for God is love"* (1 John 4:8, KJV)

- **God hates wickedness:** *"This then is the message which we have heard of him, and declare unto you, that God is light, and in him is no darkness at all"* (1 John 1:5, KJV). (Proverbs 6:16–9, KJV)
- **God cares:** *"For our God is a consuming fire"* (Hebrews 12:29, KJV). (1 Peter 5:7, KJV)
- **God grieves:** *"God is a Spirit: and they that worship him must worship him in spirit and in truth"* (John 4:24, KJV). (Genesis 6:6, KJV)

These attributes show us that God is relational and responsive to human actions and emotions.

The Nature of God

Building on our understanding of God's personality, we can delve deeper into His fundamental nature. Scripture reveals several key aspects:

- **God is love:** *"He that loveth not knows not God; for God is love"* (1 John 4:8–16, KJV).
- **God is light:** *"This then is the message which we have heard of him, and declare unto you, that God is light, and in him is no darkness at all"* (1 John 1:5, KJV).
- **God is a consuming fire:** *"For our God is a consuming fire"* (Hebrews 12:29, KJV).
- **God is a spirit:** *"God is a Spirit: and they that worship him must worship him in spirit and in truth"* (John 4:24, KJV).

These characteristics help us grasp the essence of who God is and how He interacts with His creation.

The Grace of God

A crucial aspect of God's nature is His grace. Ephesians 2:8–9 (KJV) tells us:

> *"For by grace are ye saved through faith; and that not of yourselves: it is the gift of God: Not of works, lest any man should boast."*

God's grace is His unmerited favor towards us. It's unconditional, sufficient, non-discriminatory, and transformative. Through His grace, we are saved, justified, and made heirs to His kingdom.

The Sovereignty of God

Finally, we come to God's sovereignty, His supreme power and authority over all creation. One of the most profound illustrations of God's sovereignty is found in the book of Job.

After Job and his friends have debated the reasons for Job's suffering, God Himself speaks. These rhetorical questions serve to remind Job (and us) of our limited perspective. God is pointing out that He was present and active at the very foundation of the earth, a time no human could witness. He's emphasizing the vast gap between divine and human knowledge and capabilities. His response, spanning chapters 38–41, is a series of questions that highlight His power and wisdom in contrast to human limitations.

For example, God asks Job:

> *"Where were you when I laid the foundations of the earth? Tell Me, if you have understanding. Who determined its measurements? Surely you know!"* (Job 38:4-5, KJV)

These questions continue, covering topics from the weather to wild animals, demonstrating God's intricate involvement in and control over all aspects of His creation:

> *"Then the LORD answered Job out of the whirlwind, and said: 'Who is this who darkens counsel by words without knowledge? Now prepare yourself like a man; I will question you, and you shall answer Me. Where were you when I laid the foundations of the earth? Tell Me, if you have understanding. Who determined its measurements? Surely you know! Or who stretched the line upon it? To what were its foundations fastened? Or who laid its cornerstone, when the morning stars sang together, and all the sons of God shouted for joy? Or who shut in the sea with doors, when it burst forth and issued from the womb; when I made the clouds its garment, and thick darkness its swaddling band; when I fixed My limit for it, and set bars and doors; when I said, 'This far you may come, but no farther, and here your proud waves must stop!' Have you commanded the morning since your days began, and caused the dawn to know its place, that it might take hold of the ends of the earth, and the wicked be shaken out of it? It takes on form like clay under a seal and stands out like a garment. From the wicked their light is withheld, and the upraised arm is broken. Have you entered the springs of the sea? Or have you walked in search of the depths? Have the gates of death been revealed to you? Or have you seen the doors of the shadow of death? Have you comprehended the breadth of the earth? Tell me if you know all this"* (Job 38:1–18, NKJV).

Here, God is highlighting His knowledge of the deepest parts of the sea and the mysteries of death, areas that were (and in many ways still are) beyond human exploration or understanding. This serves to further illustrate the extent of God's knowledge and control over all aspects of creation.

> *"Where is the way to the dwelling of light? And darkness, where is its place, that you may take it to its territory, that you may know the paths to its home? Do you know it, because you were born then, or because the number of your days is great? Have you entered the treasury of snow, or have you seen the treasury of hail, which I have reserved for the time of trouble, for the day of battle and war? By what way is light diffused, or the east wind scattered over the earth? Who has divided a channel for the overflowing water, or a path for the thunderbolt, to cause it to rain on a land where there is no one, a wilderness in which there is no man; to satisfy the desolate waste, and cause to spring forth the growth of tender grass? Has the rain a father? Or who has begotten the drops of dew? From whose womb comes the ice, and the frost of heaven, who gives it birth? The waters harden like stone, and the surface of the deep is frozen"* (Job 38:19–30, NKJV).

The passage goes on to cover topics from weather patterns to the behavior of various animals, all serving to demonstrate God's intricate involvement in and control over all aspects of creation. For instance:

> *"Can you bind the cluster of the Pleiades, or loose the belt of Orion? Can you bring out Mazzaroth in its season? Or can you guide the Great Bear with its cubs? Do you know the ordinances of the heavens? Can you set their dominion over the earth? Can you lift up your voice to the*

clouds, that an abundance of water may cover you? Can you send out lightning, that they may go, and say to you, 'Here we are!'? Who has put wisdom in the mind? Or who has given understanding to the heart? Who can number the clouds by wisdom? Or who can pour out the bottles of heaven, when the dust hardens in clumps, and the clods cling together?" (Job 38:31–38, NKJV)

Reading this and understanding that God created the Mazzaroth, or the constellations, when we talk about the zodiac signs, Orion and other star clusters, we know that God placed them there in accordance with His wisdom.

"Can you hunt the prey for the lion, or satisfy the appetite of the young lions, when they crouch in their dens, or lurk in their lairs to lie in wait? Who provides food for the raven, when its young ones cry to God, and wander about for lack of food? Do you know the time when the wild mountain goats bear young? Or can you mark when the deer gives birth? Can you number the months that they fulfill, or do you know the time when they bear young? They bow down, they bring forth their young, they deliver their offspring. Their young ones are healthy, they grow strong with grain; they depart and do not return to them.

Who set the wild donkey free? Who loosed the bonds of the onager, whose home I have made the wilderness, and the barren land his dwelling? He scorns the tumult of the city; he does not heed the shouts of the driver. The range of the mountains is his pasture, and he searches after every green thing.

Will the wild ox be willing to serve you? Will he bed by your manger? Can you bind the wild ox in the furrow

> *with ropes? Or will he plow the valleys behind you? Will you trust him because his strength is great? Or will you leave your labor to him? Will you trust him to bring home your grain, and gather it to your threshing floor?*
>
> *The wings of the ostrich wave proudly, but are her wings and pinions like the kindly stork's? For she leaves her eggs on the ground and warms them in the dust; she forgets that a foot may crush them, or that a wild beast may break them. She treats her young harshly, as though they were not hers; her labor is in vain, without concern, because God deprived her of wisdom, and did not endow her with understanding. When she lifts herself on high, she scorns the horse and its rider.*
>
> *Have you given the horse strength? Have you clothed his neck with thunder? Can you frighten him like a locust? His majestic snorting strikes terror. He paws in the valley and rejoices in his strength; he gallops into the clash of arms. He mocks at fear and is not frightened; nor does he turn back from the sword. The quiver rattles against him, the glittering spear and javelin. He devours the distance with fierceness and rage; nor does he come to a halt because the trumpet has sounded. At the blast of the trumpet he says, 'Aha!' He smells the battle from afar, the thunder of captains and shouting"* (Job 38:39–39:25, NKJV).

God is so good. He feeds the wild animals; how could we believe He would not care for us the same? I can appreciate the horse a lot more after reading that the horse does not cower down in the face of danger. We should be working toward not turning back when things are not going our way.

> *"Does the hawk fly by your wisdom, and spread its wings toward the south? Does the eagle mount up at your com-*

> *mand, and make its nest on high? On the rock it dwells and resides, on the crag of the rock and the stronghold. From there it spies out the prey; its eyes observe from afar. Its young ones suck up blood; and where the slain are, there it is"* (Job 38–39, KJV).

These last few questions are no different than all of the previous questions. We should ask ourselves just a few of the questions God asked Job. After God asks these questions, He finishes His address by asking this:

> *"Shall the one who contends with the Almighty correct Him? He who rebukes God, let him answer it"* (Job 40:1–2, KJV).

Wow, I had to include the whole thing. When I first read this, I was in awe. This extended dialogue serves multiple purposes: It reminds us of God's unfathomable wisdom and power; it puts human knowledge and abilities in perspective; and it challenges us to trust in God's sovereignty even when we don't understand His ways. It suggests that instead of questioning God's actions, we should marvel at His works and trust His wisdom.

By presenting God's own words in this way, the book of Job provides one of the most vivid illustrations of divine sovereignty in the Bible. It encourages us to approach God with humility, recognizing our limited understanding in the face of His infinite wisdom and power.

As we've explored these aspects of God's nature, His existence, personality, fundamental attributes, grace, and sovereignty, we begin to grasp the depth and breadth of who God is. This understanding forms the foundation for our relationship with Him and shapes how we view the world and our place in it.

In the next chapter, we'll dive deeper into how this knowledge of God impacts our daily lives and our understanding of His responses to our prayers and needs. Praise God for who He is before going to the next chapter as we prepare to discuss Moses a little further.

Self-Evaluation Questions:

- **God's Existence and Creation:** Romans 1:20 (KJV) states that God's "eternal power and Godhead" are "clearly seen" through creation. How does understanding God as Creator impact your daily relationship with Him? What aspects of creation most clearly reveal God's character to you?
- **God's Personality Revealed:** The chapter describes God as loving, hating wickedness, caring, and grieving. How does understanding that God has emotions and attitudes change your perspective on prayer and worship? Which aspect of God's personality do you most need to understand better?
- **Multiple Aspects of God's Nature:** God is described as love, light, consuming fire, and spirit. How do these seemingly different characteristics work together to form a complete picture of who God is? Why might it be important to understand all aspects rather than focusing on just one?
- **Grace in Daily Life:** Ephesians 2:8–9 (KJV) emphasizes that salvation is by grace through faith, not works. How

should understanding God's grace influence the way we approach Him with our requests and needs? How does grace relate to the concept of God always saying "Yes"?

- **God's Sovereignty Demonstrated:** The extensive passage from Job 38–41(KJV) shows God's authority over creation. How does recognizing God's sovereignty help us trust His responses to our prayers, even when we don't understand them? What questions from God's response to Job most impact your understanding of His power?

Moment of Prayer:

I praise You for being a God of emotion and relationship. You love deeply, You grieve over sin, You care tenderly for Your children, and You hate the wickedness that destroys what You have made beautiful. Forgive me for the times I have reduced You to a one-dimensional figure in my prayers. Open my heart to understand the fullness of who You are.

When I struggle to comprehend Your love, remind me of the cross. When I need to understand Your holiness, let me see Your hatred of sin. When I doubt Your care, show me Your tender mercies new every morning, in Jesus' name, Amen.

CHAPTER THREE

God's Direction, Our Decision

This chapter emphasizes the critical importance of following God's specific instructions through the lens of Moses and the water from the rock. When Moses struck the rock instead of speaking to it as God commanded, he disqualified himself from entering the Promised Land, not because God said "No," but because disobedience has consequences. The chapter draws parallels to modern-day challenges in obeying God, showing how our reactions to criticism and circumstances can lead us away from God's intended path. The key message is that following God's precise instructions leads to blessing, while deviation leads to missed opportunities.

The Importance of Following God's Instructions

When Faith Meets Impatience

Following God's guidance brings blessings, while rushing ahead of His plan often leads to painful consequences. My story from Germany taught me this truth in a way I'll never forget.

Prayer Without Preparation

I was stationed in Germany, desperately praying for a wife. Looking back, I realize how unprepared I was for what I was asking. I had no money, no home to offer, survived on a meal card, and, most critically, I lacked faith. Yet I kept asking God, believing I could request anything from Him. We have been taught to BAG (Blab and Grab) the blessings of God.

Taking Matters into My Own Hands

Impatience got the better of me. Instead of waiting for God's timing, I decided to find a wife myself... at the local club. I met an attractive young woman and pursued her, though our relationship began on shaky ground. She revealed she already had a boyfriend but offered to make me her "lover." I countered with my own misguided proposal: "I'll be your boyfriend and let the other guy be your lover." (You could probably put a good emoji here for my ridiculous counteroffer.)

What followed were nine months of pure torment. We argued daily over trivial matters. She lived with her sister and brother-in-law, so I'd sneak through windows at night to avoid disturbing them. When I moved to new quarters where guests were restricted due to my work position, she could only visit occasionally. Every day felt like a battle.

Finally, I desperately prayed for clarity. I brought my frustration to the Lord: "God, if this is my wife, please fix our relationship so we can stop arguing every day. But if she's not the one for me, please show me clearly so I don't string her along." I knew I needed to get right with God, though I mistakenly believed I needed a wife to do it.

Within ten minutes of finishing that prayer, maybe less, came a knock at my door. There she stood. We sat down, and she said, "I want to talk to you. I don't think we should get married."

My immediate thought was, "Lord, that's too quick!" I had expected maybe a week-long process, not this sudden, cold resolution. We agreed to remain friends, but God knew even that wouldn't work, friendship could easily become "friends with benefits."

A week or so later, she had to return to the United States. Those final two weeks were rough as I wrestled with thoughts of pursuing salvation alone. On departure day, we were running late for her flight to the U.S. from Frankfurt. We were in Nuremberg, about an hour's drive on the autobahn. We barely made it in time.

These were the pre-9/11 days, so I could walk her to the gate. After a quick kiss, she promised, "I'll call you!" Then she disappeared onto the plane. That was the last time I saw her. We didn't speak again until a brief exchange on social media over a decade later.

The Burden Lifted

As I was walking away from that terminal, something remarkable happened. As I moved down the conveyor walkway, I felt a tremendous burden lift from my shoulders. I felt myself growing taller, spiritually speaking. At that moment, I returned to the Lord with clear vision.

I found a church and rededicated my life on Resurrection Sunday, 1988. I've been walking with God ever since, and I remember that day as clearly as if it were yesterday. Those nine months of turmoil and anguish were the direct consequence of my impatience, of trying to do God's work for Him instead of trusting His timing. When we ask the Lord something, we must prepare ourselves and trust His guidance when He says, "Here I come."

The choice is ours: trust in the Lord's perfect timing or suffer the consequences of running ahead of His plan.

This chapter explores the critical nature of heeding God's direction and the impact of our decisions.

Biblical Example: Moses and the Water from the Rock

When God gave specific instructions to Moses about how He would yield water from a rock, let's look at how that played out in the book of Numbers 20 (ESV):

> *"Then came the children of Israel, even the whole congregation, into the desert of Zin in the first month: and the people abode in Kadesh; and Miriam died there and was buried there. And there was no water for the congregation: and they gathered themselves together against Moses and against Aaron.*
>
> *And the people chode with Moses, and spoke, saying, 'Would God that we had died when our brethren died before the Lord! And why have ye brought up the congregation of the Lord into this wilderness, that we and our cattle should die there? And wherefore have ye made us to come up out of Egypt, to bring us in unto this evil place? It is no place of seed, or of figs, or of vines, or of pomegranates; neither is there any water to drink.'*

And Moses and Aaron went from the presence of the assembly unto the door of the tabernacle of the congregation, and they fell upon their faces: and the glory of the Lord appeared unto them.

And the Lord spoke unto Moses, saying, 'Take the rod, and gather thou the assembly together, thou, and Aaron thy brother, and speak ye unto the rock before their eyes; and it shall give forth his water, and thou shalt bring forth to them water out of the rock: so thou shalt give the congregation and their beasts drink.'

And Moses took the rod from before the Lord, as he commanded him."

"And Moses and Aaron gathered the congregation together before the rock, and he said unto them, 'Hear now, ye rebels; must we fetch you water out of this rock?' And Moses lifted up his hand, and with his rod he smote the rock twice: and the water came out abundantly, and the congregation drank, and their beasts also."

"And the Lord spoke unto Moses and Aaron, 'Because ye believed me not, to sanctify me in the eyes of the children of Israel, therefore ye shall not bring this congregation into the land which I have given them.' This is the water of Meribah; because the children of Israel strove with the Lord, and he was sanctified in them" (Numbers 20:9-13, KJV).

I don't want to get these verses confused with the first water provision in Exodus 17:1-7, where God instructed Moses to strike the rock in Horeb. Moses had been in this situation before. It was what we say, *"not his first rodeo."*

Because Moses did not follow the instructions of God and struck the rock and did not speak to the rock, he disqualified himself from God's deliverance into the Promised Land. In our lives, it is our actions, or our failure to act in situations, that keep us from the "Yes" blessings of God.

> *"Then the Lord spoke to Moses and Aaron, 'Because you did not believe Me, to hallow Me in the eyes of the children of Israel, therefore you shall not bring this assembly into the land which I have given them.' That water was called Meribah, or translated means strife or contention, because the children of Israel struggled with the Lord, and He showed Himself holy among them"* (Numbers 20:7-13, ESV).

Let's Break Down What Just Happened:

First, The Setting in Numbers 20:

We find the Israelites in the desert of Zin, facing a severe water shortage. The people complain to Moses and Aaron about their predicament, like a hungry newborn.

If you remember my truth, I "cried" to the Lord about wan-ting to be married. And maybe you have cried to the Lord about something. I know I am not the only one here. I justified my action by saying, "He who finds a wife finds a good thing and obtains favor from the Lord" (Proverbs 18:22, ESV). I used that scripture, but I went looking in the wrong places. I went to a nightclub, and my motive was wrong. I really wanted to go to the club, and because I lacked the understanding of the scripture and the nature of God, I thought, *let me help God.* I later realized that I was frustrated at the situation of not having a wife and felt like that was the only way I could do God's will. I thought I would not be able to keep myself.

Second, God's Instructions to Moses:

The instructions to Moses were to take his rod; gather the assembly; speak to the rock before their eyes; and bring forth water from the rock.

In my situation, I asked God for a wife. My body was screaming at me, "I need, I need." The Lord instructed me to prepare for my wife, save money, buy key items, have a plan for a place to stay. The pressure was so strong, and doing all of that just seemed too long. I went out to get one myself, using the Bible for justification to do what I wanted to do, go find one, fulfill my desire.

Third, Moses' Actions:

Despite having previously experienced a similar situation, Moses deviates from God's instructions: he gathers the assembly before the rock; speaks harshly to the people, calling them "rebels," and strikes the rock twice with his rod instead of speaking to the rock as instructed by God.

About now you are probably thinking, "His biblical example makes no sense." Before you finish that thought, consider this: my body, my flesh, was in "the desert and thirsty." I will spell it out, I needed some lovin' but did not want to step out on God. I thought that if I found this "good thing," I would be okay.

Finally, The Consequence:

Because of this disobedience, Moses is barred from entering the Promised Land. The incident becomes known as the waters of Meribah, marking a place of contention between Israel and God.

Personal Application: Modern-Day Challenges in Obeying God

Recognizing God's Instructions

God often provides specific guidance in our lives, but we must be attuned to His voice to recognize it. Take a minute to look back at a few times when God instructed you to do something, and the action would have given God the glory. But when you executed the action, the result made you popular, wealthier, or even the next internet sensation. In turn, you used that moment of popularity or wealth as an opportunity to promote yourself.

Common Pitfalls in Obedience

There may have been times when we have allowed past experiences to override current instructions. Listening to a lot of negative talk as Moses did, people lying on you or falsely accusing you, and now you are focused on "the haters" rather than hearing what God's original instructions were to you. There will be times when God will instruct you to: keep your mouth shut, sit still and let Him work it out, or even walk away from a situation.

Whichever scenario you fall into, when God instructs you in how to deal with it and you take it upon yourself to handle it the way you feel at that time, and you lash out at someone or act out of character, you will suffer the consequence for that action.

In reacting to negative circumstances and criticism, there have been many times when God has instructed me in situations, and I heard what I wanted to hear. God would tell me to "be quiet, I will handle it." You know what I would hear?

"Handle it." I would be so into myself and my feelings that all I heard was the "handle it" part. After I handled it the way that I felt it should be done, I would go back to the Lord and wonder why it didn't go over the way I thought it should have resolved. After a shellacking from the Lord, the Lord would tell me where I stopped following His instruction and carried out my own.

The Importance of a Relationship with God

To accurately discern God's instructions, we must cultivate a close relationship with Him. In every situation that didn't go as we thought it should go, we can normally trace it back to God telling us to stop, be still, be quiet, be... just be obedient to God's instruction.

For a positive outcome, it is important to listen to God's voice. How do we know God's instruction from the persuader's counterfeit solutions? You must know God's voice. How do you know God's voice? You must know Him.

We talked about the existence of God. You must have a relationship with God and know His Son and what God did through Jesus for us all. Looking to Jesus as an example, Jesus' life and teachings provide a perfect model for following God's instructions and maintaining a close relationship with the Father. When you know the life and walk of Jesus, the knowledge will make following the instructions of God easier. In the next chapter, we will look at the life and walk of Jesus.

Self-Evaluation Questions:

- **Learning from Mistakes:** I shared my painful experience of trying to find a wife in the wrong places with wrong motives. What lessons can you extract about the consequences of taking matters into your own hands instead of waiting on God's timing?

- **Moses' Disobedience:** In Numbers 20, Moses struck the rock instead of speaking to it as God instructed, which cost him entry into the Promised Land. How does this story illustrate the importance of following God's specific instructions rather than relying on past experiences?
- **Recognizing God's Instructions:** I mentioned times when God told me to «be quiet, I will handle it,» but I only heard «handle it.» How can you better tune your spiritual ears to hear complete instructions rather than selective hearing based on your emotions?
- **Relationship and Obedience:** The chapter emphasizes that accurately discerning God's instructions requires a close relationship with Him. What practical steps can you take to deepen your relationship with God so you can better recognize His voice?
- **Past Experience vs. Present Guidance:** Moses had successfully struck a rock before, but God's instructions were different this time. How can you avoid the trap of assuming God will always work the same way He has in the past? What's the balance between learning from experience and staying open to new direction?

Moment of Prayer:

You are love that embraces, light that illuminates, consuming fire that purifies, and spirit that transcends all understanding. I con-

fess that sometimes I try to limit You to just one aspect, seeking only Your comfort without Your correction, desiring Your blessings without Your holiness, wanting Your presence without surrendering to Your Lordship.

Help me to embrace the beautiful complexity of who You are, knowing that each attribute works in perfect harmony with the others for my good and Your glory. In Jesus' name I thank you.

Amen.

CHAPTER FOUR

Relationship with Jesus

Essential to understanding God's "Yes" is knowing Jesus Christ, who claimed "all power in heaven and earth." This comprehensive chapter covers Jesus' humanity (experiencing hunger, thirst, temptation without sin); His virgin birth (the biological miracle that made God incarnate), His life and ministry (preaching, healing, performing miracles); His vicarious death (natural, unnatural, preternatural, and supernatural); His resurrection (with many infallible proofs); and His ascension and promised return.

The chapter concludes with a clear presentation of the gospel and God's sevenfold plan of salvation, establishing the foundation for believers to understand their authority and relationship with God.

The Introduction of Jesus Christ

Jesus Christ is the Son of God. He claimed to have *"all power in heaven and in earth,"* as found in the gospel book of Matthew 28:18 (KJV). He walked upon the blue waters of Galilee. The winds and the waves obeyed His command. He healed the sick and raised the dead. He gave sight to the blind and hearing to the deaf. He cast out demons and made the lame walk. He turned water into wine and fed more than five thousand with five loaves of bread and two fish. Remember, there were some leftovers.

I would be remiss if I did not take the opportunity to talk about the humanity and incarnation of Jesus Christ, the concept that God became human in the person of Jesus Christ: His birth, walk, death, and resurrection. Then you will be able to understand that when you are a child of God, in the will of God, like Jesus, there is nothing you can't ask, and it be done for you. The fact is, Jesus did not waste His words by asking God to do just anything, like a genie in a bottle.

The Humanity of Jesus Christ

The humanity of Jesus Christ is seen in His human parentage and development as a normal human being. He was subject to all the sinless infirmities of human nature. Matthew records Jesus as being hungry; John records Him as being thirsty and tired; and He cried. In the book of Hebrews 4:15 (KJV), Jesus was tempted but never budged. Jesus is man, and yet He is more than man. He is not God and man, but He is the God-man. He is God in human flesh. His two natures are bound together in a way that the two become one, having a single consciousness and will.

The Life of Jesus Christ

His virgin birth cannot be paralleled in the history of mankind. It was by the virgin birth that God became man. Two natures, one perfect person, one being almighty God, and the other being man without sin. The two natures became Christ Jesus.

In the third chapter of Genesis, the introduction of His virgin birth is told. The one to defeat Satan was to be of the seed of the woman. This is a biological miracle; in the Scripture, Mary "knew" no man, she was a virgin. In Luke 1:34-35 (KJV), we understand that He was of a woman and without a human father.

This birth was prophesied in Isaiah: a *"virgin would conceive and bear a son and shall call His name Immanuel (God with us)."* He also prophesied, *"Unto us a child is born, unto us a son is given."* This means that God gave His only begotten Son who was with Him from eternity, and the child Jesus was born of a virgin. God gave His Son unto us (Isaiah 9:6-7, KJV). He was born in Bethlehem (Micah 5:2, KJV). Joseph with Mary went up to Bethlehem to be taxed and to fulfill prophecy (Luke 2:1–7, KJV).

He walked among us, preaching, healing, and telling us what was to come, that He would soon be crucified for our sins.

The Death of Jesus Christ

His death is mentioned in the New Testament and is spoken of many times by the prophets in the Old Testament. His death was vicarious and was God's substitute for our sins. On the cross, Christ was made sin for the sinner. By faith in Him, we are made righteous with the righteousness of God. You can read this and more in the book of Matthew 20 and 2 Corinthians 5.

The death of Jesus Christ was natural, unnatural, preternatural, and supernatural.

By a natural death, His spirit and soul were separated from His body. This can be found in John 19.

An unnatural death is a death that is caused by external forces. He was sinless, which means He committed no crime or sin, in that He *"did no sin"* (Romans 6:23, KJV), (1 Peter 2:22, KJV), *"had no sin"* (1 John 3:5, KJV), or *"knew no sin"* (2 Corinthians 5:21, KJV). Before He could die, He had to be "made sin" for us. Therefore, His death was unnatural.

His preternatural death means that the death of Jesus Christ was not an afterthought with God; it was forethought of God (Revelation 13:8, KJV).

The supernatural death of Jesus Christ was *"No man taketh life from me."* In John 10:18 (KJV), He said, *"I lay it down of myself"* (supernaturally). *"I have power to take it up again"* (supernaturally). This He did on the cross, and three days and three nights later, He took life up again when He rose from the dead.

Only God in the form of man could die a vicarious (suffering on behalf of humanity), natural, unnatural, preternatural (beyond what is natural or normal), and supernatural death.

The Resurrection of Jesus Christ

The doctrine of every disciple was the resurrection of Jesus Christ, the faith of every believer, and should be the theme of every sermon.

In John 11:25 (KJV), Jesus said, *"I am the resurrection and the life."* Luke tells us in Acts 1:3 (KJV) that we have "many infallible proofs" of His resurrection, evidence that cannot be mistaken or doubted.

According to the witnesses in the 20th chapter of John, He first appeared to Mary Magdalene, and Thomas also had an encounter with Jesus, as well as the seven by the sea of Tiberias. Jesus appeared to Peter and the Emmaus disciples in Luke the 24th chapter. He was seen by James and over five hundred other brethren in First Corinthians 15. In Matthew, the 28th chapter, the eleven apostles saw Jesus. And in Acts, the 7th through 9th chapters, Stephen, the first martyr, and Paul on the way to Damascus experienced Jesus.

The Ascension and Second Coming of Jesus Christ

The bodily rising of Jesus into heaven after His resurrection, called the ascension of Jesus, can be found in Hebrews 10, where He ascended on high and sits at the right hand of God.

His second coming is when Jesus returns to this earth in the future, as was foretold in Acts, the first chapter. This same Jesus that ascended into heaven will so come in the same manner.

The message of the Second Coming of Jesus is so important that it is mentioned over three hundred times in the New Testament. A few references are: He is coming to take His Church to be with Him (1 Thessalonians 4, KJV); He is coming to judge the nations (Matthew 25, KJV); He is coming to save Israel (Romans 11, KJV); He is coming to sit upon the throne of David (Luke 1, KJV). He is coming to bring righteous government to this earth. Jesus Christ is coming back to this earth again. Take this time to evaluate your life. Where you are right now, will you be ready when Jesus comes for you? God will not reject you now.

Being a Child of God

Being a child of God is important. Here are some truths to know before going forward. It is important that you accept

Jesus as your Lord and Savior. Doing this will help you understand your authority, responsibility, and the will of God for your life.

Take this time to reflect and know that there is only one way and that is God's way; and God's way is a person, and that person is His Son, the Lord Jesus Christ (John 14:6, KJV). Jesus Christ appeared on earth to save you from the three "P's":

- The **penalty** of sin (Hebrews 9:26, KJV).
- He appeared in heaven, in the presence of God, after His resurrection, to save you from the **power** of sin (Hebrews 9:24, KJV).
- He will appear again on this earth, the second time, as "Lord of Lords" and "King of Kings," to save you from the very **presence** of sin (Hebrews 9:28, KJV).

God's Salvation Is Threefold

There are **seven facts** revealed in God's plan for our salvation, being saved from the consequences of sin and reconciled to God. As you study them, keep in mind that this is God's plan, not man's, it is God's. *There is no other plan that can save your lost soul and make you a child of God* (Acts 4:12, KJV).

1. It Is a Fact That God Loves You. *"For God so loved the world, that he gave his only begotten Son, that whosoever believeth in him should not perish, but have everlasting life"* (John 3:16, KJV).

Jesus Christ was made for that which God hates, sin, that you might be made that which God loves, righteousness. **Because God so loves you, you can exchange your sins for**

His righteousness. Calvary is proof that God loves and longs to save you.

2. It Is a Fact That You Are a Sinner. "*For all have sinned, and come short of the glory of God*" (Romans 3:23, KJV).

a) Sin is the transgression of the law, "*Whosoever committeth sin transgresseth also the law: for sin is the transgression of the law*" (1 John 3:4, KJV).

b) Sin is unbelief; it calls God a liar. "*He that believeth on the Son of God hath the witness in himself: he that believeth not God hath made him a liar; because he believeth not the record that God gave of his Son*" (1 John 5:10, KJV).

c) Sin is active rebellion against God. "*Hear, O heavens, and give ear, O earth: for the Lord hath spoken, I have nourished and brought up children, and they have rebelled against me*" (Isaiah 1:2, KJV).

d) Sin is passive (not active) rebellion against God. "*Therefore to him that knoweth to do good, and doeth it not, to him it is sin*" (James 4:17, KJV).

e) All unrighteousness is sin. "*All unrighteousness is sin: and there is a sin not unto death*" (1 John 5:17, KJV).

3. It Is a Fact That You Are Now Dead in Sin. "*For the wages of sin is death; but the gift of God is eternal life through Jesus Christ our Lord*" (Romans 6:23, KJV).

You are dead in sin until you accept Christ as your personal Savior. The apostle Paul said, "*You hath he quickened (made alive, especially in a spiritual sense), who were dead in trespasses and sins*" (Ephesians 2:1, KJV). To be saved is to be made spiritually alive in Christ.

What is death?

a) Death is **spiritual** separation. Your sins have separated you from God.

b) Death is **physical** separation. It separates the spirit and the soul from the body.

c) Death is **eternal** separation. If you remain lost in your sins, you will stand before God at the great white throne of judgment, and there your sins will separate you from the mercy of God forever; this is hell.

4. It Is a Fact That Christ Died for You. *"For when we were yet without strength, in due time Christ died for the ungodly. For scarcely for a righteous man will one die: yet peradventure for a good man some would even dare to die. But God commendeth his love toward us, in that, while we were yet sinners, Christ died for us"* (Romans 5:6–8, KJV).

a) *"For he (God the Father) hath made him (God the Son) to be sin for us..."* (2 Corinthians 5:21, KJV).

b) *"Forasmuch as ye know that ye were not redeemed with corruptible things..."* (1 Peter 1:18–19, KJV).

c) *"For Christ also hath once suffered for sins..."* (1 Peter 3:18, KJV).

d) *"Christ died for our sins..."* (1 Corinthians 15:3, KJV).

5. It Is a Fact That You Can Be Saved By Faith In The Lord Jesus Christ. *"...Believe on the Lord Jesus Christ, and thou shalt be saved, and thy house"* (Acts 16:30-31, KJV).

The gospel, or "Good News," saves when you believe:

a) It is that Christ died for our sins.

b) He was buried.

c) He rose again on the third day. "*...how that Christ died for our sins according to the scriptures; and that he was buried, and that he rose again the third day according to the scriptures*" (1 Corinthians 15:3–4, KJV).

d) The gospel is the power of God unto salvation only when you believe. *"For I am not ashamed of the gospel of Christ: for it is the power of God unto salvation to every one that believeth; to the Jew first, and also to the Greek"* (Romans 1:16, KJV). Your faith in Jesus Christ releases the power of God that saves your soul.

e) "*When you confess with your mouth...*" (Romans 10:9–10, KJV).

Accept Him now by faith and pray this prayer:

"Lord Jesus, I know you love me, because you died on the cross bearing my sins. Thank you, Lord, for revealing to me my sinful condition. I confess that I am a sinner, dead in sin and cannot save myself. I do now, by faith, accept you as my personal Savior and thank you for eternal salvation, Amen."

6. You Can Have a New Life and Know It. *"These things have I written unto you that believe on the name of the Son of God; that ye may know that ye have eternal life, and that ye may believe on the name of the Son of God"* (1 John 5:13, KJV). Your faith in God's infallible Word is your assurance of salvation.

a) That you are now a child of God. *"Beloved, now are we the sons of God, and it doth not yet appear what we shall be: but we know that, when he shall appear, we shall be like him; for we shall see him as he is"* (1 John 3:2, KJV).

b) That you have been made the righteousness of God in Christ. *"Therefore if any man be in Christ, he is a new creature: old things are passed away; behold, all things are become new"* (2 Corinthians 5:21, KJV) and *"For Christ is the end of the law for righteousness to every one that believeth"* (Romans 10:4, KJV).

c) That you are a new creature in Christ. *"Therefore if any man be in Christ, he is a new creature: old things are passed away; behold, all things are become new"* (2 Corinthians 5:17, KJV).

d) That you are now a son and heir of God. *"Wherefore thou art no more a servant, but a son; and if a son, then an heir of God through Christ"* (Galatians 4:7, KJV).

7. It Is a Fact That You Are Now a Child of God and You Are to Obey Him. *"Then Peter and the other apostles answered and said, We ought to obey God rather than men"* (Acts 5:29, KJV)

Determine how to obey your Lord and Master, Jesus Christ, in all things.

a) Unite with a New Testament church. *"Praising God, and having favour with all the people. And the Lord added to the church daily such as should be saved"* (Acts 2:47, KJV).

b) Follow Him in the ordinance of baptism. *"Then they that gladly received his word were baptized: and the same day there were added unto them about three thousand souls"* (Acts 2:41, KJV).

c) Join a Sunday school or Bible Study class and study the Word with God's children. *"Study to shew thyself approved unto God, a workman that needeth not to be ashamed, rightly dividing the word of truth* (2 Timothy 2:15, KJV).

d) Attend the worship services of your church. *"Not forsaking the assembling of ourselves together, as the manner of some is; but exhorting one another: and so much the more, as ye see the day approaching"* (Hebrews 10:25, KJV).

e) Be a faithful steward. *"Moreover it is required in stewards, that a man be found faithful"* (1 Corinthians 4:2, KJV)

> *"What? know ye not that your body is the temple of the Holy Ghost which is in you, which ye have of God, and ye are not your own? For ye are bought with a price: therefore glorify God in your body, and in your spirit, which are God's"* (1 Corinthians 6:19–20, KJV).
>
> *"Bring ye all the tithes into the storehouse, that there may be meat in mine house, and prove me now herewith, saith the Lord of hosts, if I will not open you the windows of heaven, and pour you out a blessing, that there shall not be room enough to receive it"* (Malachi 3:10, KJV).

f) Make time in your daily life to pray and read God's Word.

Self-Evaluation Questions:

- **Jesus' Humanity and Divinity:** The chapter describes Jesus as both fully human (experiencing hunger, thirst, and temptation) and fully divine. How does understanding both natures of Christ impact your relationship with Him? Why is it important that Jesus experienced human limitations?
- **The Purpose of Jesus' Death:** This chapter describes Jesus' death as «natural, unnatural, preternatural, and supernatural.» How does understanding the multifaceted nature of

Christ's death deepen your appreciation for salvation? What does it mean that He «laid down» His life voluntarily?

- **Evidence of the Resurrection:** Multiple witnesses saw Jesus after His resurrection, from Mary Magdalene to over 500 brethren. Why is the resurrection central to Christian faith? How does the reality of the resurrection change how we approach life and prayer?
- **Jesus' Second Coming:** The chapter mentions that the Second Coming is referenced over 300 times in the New Testament. How should the promise of Christ's return influence our daily decisions and priorities? Are you ready for His return?
- **The Plan of Salvation:** Review the seven facts of God's salvation plan outlined in the chapter. Which aspect of salvation do you find most meaningful or challenging to understand? How does accepting Jesus as Lord and Savior relate to receiving God's «Yes» in prayer?

A Moment of Prayer:

Thank you that my salvation rests not on my works, but on Your grace alone through faith. Let this truth transform how I approach You in prayer, not as one trying to earn Your favor, but as a beloved child coming to a loving Father.

Help me understand that Your grace doesn't just save me; it sustains me, guides me, and empowers me to live for Your glory. When I pray, remind me that Your "Yes" flows from Your gracious heart, not from my performance.

It's You, Lord, that I put my trust. In the matchless name of Jesus, Amen.

CHAPTER FIVE

The Yes of David

David's Fall

Through David's fall with Bathsheba, this chapter illustrates God's forgiveness and redirection rather than rejection. David's absence from his post (the battlefield) led to temptation, sin, cover-up, and consequences. However, when David desired to build a temple for God, God didn't say "No." Instead, He redirected this honor to Solomon.

The chapter emphasizes examining our motives when asking God for anything, showing how God can fulfill our godly desires through different means than we expect. David's story demonstrates that even after serious sin, God's fundamental response to His repentant children remains affirmative when their hearts align with His purposes.

The last few chapters were intense, I understand that. However, we needed to know our Lord and Savior before we jumped into understanding God's responses to our desires. David's "Yes" is an example of a forgiving God. We'll see that even when he left his post, his assignment, he chose to get back on his post.

The Setting

When I say, "his post," I am referring to the watchman in Ezekiel 33. When we are not guarding our actions, thoughts, and habits, we tend to be more vulnerable to the enemy's actions and plots to derail us.

David was a man after God's own heart. He was a great warrior who started as a shepherd and eventually became a king of battle who would spend seasons out on the battlefield. This time, King David remained in the city while his men went out to battle.

He was on the balcony one day and saw Bathsheba, one of his best warriors' wives, out taking a bath. Listen, we think temptation comes to find us, well, sometimes we walk into it because of our own desires.

When you read this truth about David, wonder about this: they did not recently build a wash area, and he didn't build his palace by the bath area. The only way he was able to see Bathsheba taking a bath was by not being out on the battlefield.

The Sin

We don't just wake up and sin. There is a process to sinning, a crescendo, if you will. This happened while her husband was at war. David's desires made the temptation intolerable, and he sent for her.

After "knowing her" the Bible way, she became pregnant, and he tried to cover up his sin by bringing Uriah, Bathsheba's husband, back from the battlefield, hoping he would be intimate with his wife, and it would look like the baby was his child. Uriah was a loyal man and refused to sleep with his wife while his men were still on the battlefield.

The Cover-Up

In David's final attempt to cover his wrongdoing, he gave orders for Uriah to be placed on the front lines in a battle where he knew he would likely be killed, and he was. Nathan, the prophet, rebuked David for his sin and said God would forgive David, but his child would not survive.

The Consequences

There is forgiveness for our sins, and with our sins come consequences. We usually know, if we are believers, when we are tempted. When we don't stay vigilant, we are drawn away by our own lust.

I encourage you to read the facts of David's infraction and how it affected others around him. David asked God if he could build a temple for Him. God informed David that he would not be able to build the temple because there was too much blood on his hands. David was a man of war, and God wanted a man of peace to build the temple.

There was no double jeopardy referring to David's infraction, he had already been chastened for the Bathsheba incident. When we ask God for something and we don't get it when we think we should, or it doesn't come to pass, do not think God said "No," or He did not hear you because of a past sin that we have committed and later repented from. Instead, hear from God to see how He will bring it to pass.

He Says Yes!

God is faithful and hears our prayers, our requests, and our desires. David had an unselfish desire to build a permanent temple for the Ark of the Covenant rather than a tent. That was for the upbuilding of God's kingdom. God did not say "No." Instead, He allowed David's son to build the temple. God answered the prayer of David.

Some believe God said no to David. We can't see it that way. What I do see is where a temple was built for the Ark of the Covenant.

This is one of the reasons he was one after God's heart. David just wanted the temple built; it was not about him but about God.

If you are a believer who has been asking God for something and you feel like He is not answering you or said no, I encourage you to think about what you are asking Him for. More importantly, why do you want it? What is the reason? What is your motive?

For instance, if you are asking God for a child so you can feel like a woman, you may not have had one, but there are many children who need homes and families.

Your Motive

You must check your motive for whatever you are asking God for. If you want to be rich, why?

There was a student who wanted to be a great pro football player. When asked why, he said so he could be rich and have all the women. The whole stardom scene will take him on a course that will be very difficult to return from. What is your motive?

Do you want prestige? There was a woman who said she wanted to reach the top of her corporation so she could show everybody that she could run things as a woman and no one could tell her what to do. What is your motive?

Do you feel incomplete? A woman may desire a child to feel complete or feel like a woman. What is your motive? You may find that your calling is to raise or foster children, nieces or nephews, to give them the experience of love the way you know God.

You may even find out you were not cut out for the task. What is your motive?

The motive of a couple I know was that they wanted children. Naturally or adopted, they just wanted to raise children. They could not have children on their own, but they started fostering children. The first children they fostered, they adopted. The children even look like them. God has a way of doing that when your motive points to him.

I am a parent of an adopted child, and I am aware of the horror stories surrounding getting attached to a foster child or children, and the fear that they will go back to their natural parents one day. That is simply not always the case.

The children of that couple were blessings to the couple, but better than that, the parents have been a blessing to those children. For years, they could take nieces and nephews back home to their parents when they got tired of them, but these adopted children, the couple could not give back or take them back home, they were home.

The couple had to plow through the rough terrain of parenting to get to the pasture of praise!

What is your motive? Answer the why, does it line up with the will of God?

Before we move on to the next chapter dealing with guidance, I want to be clear about being at your post. A better word may be to be vigilant of distractions, to be on the lookout for counterfeit solutions and forged fake faith. I am not instructing us to go out and take matters into our own hands.

David was drawn away from his post by lust. We are often drawn away by our lust, maybe not a beautiful woman or handsome man, but by our children and jobs. We often do that, try to do things ourselves or get it done through all means necessary to achieve *our* desire.

In these last examples of the "Yes," I am saying that we need to check our motive. If our desires are self-centered, our tendency is to get angry with God and leave our post. We must pray for guidance, hear God, and move as He says to move. When we do this, we will find that God already has our back.

Self-Evaluation Questions:

- **David's Failure and Restoration:** Despite David's serious sin with Bathsheba and against Uriah, he's still called «a man after God's own heart.» What does this teach us about God's forgiveness and restoration? How can we maintain our relationship with God after significant failures?
- **Consequences vs. Punishment:** David faced consequences for his actions (the death of his child, not being allowed to build the temple) even after receiving forgiveness. How

do we distinguish between God's discipline and punishment? Why might there be consequences even after repentance?

- **The Temple Request:** When David wanted to build God's temple, God allowed his son Solomon to fulfill this desire instead. How was this actually a "Yes" rather than a "No"? What does this teach us about God's timing and methods?
- **Examining Our Motives:** The chapter challenges us to examine why we want what we're asking for. Using the examples given (wanting children to «feel like a woman» or wanting success to prove something), how can we honestly assess our motivations in prayer?
- **Staying on Your Post:** David's troubles began when he stayed home from battle instead of being where he should have been. What does it mean to «stay on your post» in your current life situation? How does vigilance help us avoid temptation and maintain our walk with God?

A Moment of Prayer:

Like Job, I stand in awe of Your questions: "Where were you when I laid the foundations of the earth?" Your sovereignty over the morning stars, the depths of the sea, the weather patterns, and every living creature humbles me completely.

When I cannot understand Your ways, when Your timing seems too slow, when Your methods appear unclear, help me remember that You are the God who commands the dawn and sets boundaries for the seas.

Give me the wisdom to trust Your sovereign plan even when I cannot see the full picture. Help me to pray with the confidence that You hear me, the humility to submit to Your will, and the faith to believe that Your "Yes" is always working for my ultimate good and Your eternal glory.

I pray with thanksgiving, trust, and in Jesus' name, thank You. Amen.

CHAPTER SIX

God Could Have Said No

This chapter examines times when God warned of consequences but still granted requests, using Israel's demand for a king and my personal experience buying an unnecessary car in Europe. When Israel demanded a king despite God's warnings about the consequences, God granted their request while clearly outlining what would happen. Similarly, my desire for a car (influenced by comparison with others) led to an expensive lesson. The chapter teaches that God often allows us to have what we want even when it's not His best, but He always provides guidance and warnings. The key is learning to listen carefully to God's counsel and consider long-term consequences.

God will always warn you of danger and guide you toward blessings. He will never lead you astray. The key is to not just listen but to take heed. However, when our desires are strong and not in check, they can prevent us from hearing God's instructions, moving in the direction of our answers, and even lead to the destruction of our faith.

Biblical Example: Israel Demands a King

Let's look at 1 Samuel 8:4-22 (KJV). Israel demanded a king.

"Now it came to pass when Samuel was old that he made his sons judges over Israel. The name of his firstborn was Joel, and the name of his second, Abijah; they were judges in Beersheba. But his sons did not walk in his ways; they turned aside after dishonest gain, took bribes, and perverted justice."

"Then all the elders of Israel gathered and came to Samuel at Ramah, and said to him, 'Look, you are old, and your sons do not walk in your ways. Now make us a king to judge us like all the nations.'"

"But the thing displeased Samuel when they said, 'Give us a king to judge us.' So Samuel prayed to the Lord. And the Lord said to Samuel, 'Heed the voice of the people in all that they say to you; for they have not rejected you, but they have rejected Me, that I should not reign over them. According to all the works which they have done since the day that I brought them up out of Egypt, even to this day, with which they have forsaken Me and served other gods, so they are doing to you also. Now therefore, heed their voice. However, you shall solemnly forewarn them and show them the behavior of the king who will reign over them.'"

"So Samuel told all the words of the Lord to the people who asked him for a king. And he said, 'This will be the behavior of the king who will reign over you: He will take your sons and appoint them for his own chariots and to be his horsemen, and some will run before his chariots. He will appoint captains over his thousands and captains over

his fifties, will set some to plow his ground and reap his harvest, and some to make his weapons of war and equipment for his chariots. He will take your daughters to be perfumers, cooks, and bakers. And he will take the best of your fields, your vineyards, and your olive groves, and give them to his servants. He will take a tenth of your grain and your vintage, and give it to his officers and servants. And he will take your male servants, your female servants, your finest young men, and your donkeys, and put them to his work. He will take a tenth of your sheep. And you will be his servants. And you will cry out in that day because of your king whom you have chosen for yourselves, and the Lord will not hear you in that day.'"

"Nevertheless, the people refused to obey the voice of Samuel; and they said, 'No, but we will have a king over us, that we also may be like all the nations, and that our king may judge us and go out before us and fight our battles.'"

"And Samuel heard all the words of the people, and he repeated them in the hearing of the Lord. So the Lord said to Samuel, 'Heed their voice, and make them a king.' And Samuel said to the men of Israel, 'Every man go to his city.'"

This is a powerful example of wanting something so badly that we disregard God's warnings and direction. The children of Israel demanded a king, desiring to be like other nations. God didn't give a "no." He warned them, through the prophet Samuel, about the consequences of their request.

Samuel, following God's instructions, told the people:

- The king would conscript their sons for his army and labor (1 Samuel 8:11-12, KJV).

- He would take their daughters as servants (1 Samuel 8:13, KJV).
- He would seize their best fields and vineyards (1 Samuel 8:14, KJV).
- He would impose taxes on their produce and flocks (1 Samuel 8:15–17, KJV).
- They would become servants to the king (1 Samuel 8:17, KJV).

Despite these warnings, the people insisted, saying, *"No! But there shall be a king over us, that we also may be like all the nations, and that our king may judge us and go out before us and fight our battles"* (1 Samuel 8:19–20, KJV).

God ultimately granted their request, demonstrating that He allows us to have what we want, even if it's not in our best interest.

Personal Example: The Car I Didn't Need

When I lived in Europe, I experienced a similar situation. Despite having access to excellent public transportation, I desperately wanted a car. My desire blinded me to reason and God's guidance.

One day, I walked into a car dealership where a saleswoman approached me, asking, "May I help you find a car?" Excited, I replied, "Yes." I left with a Nissan Sentra and a large car payment. Ironically, I didn't even have a license to drive the car at the time (1 Samuel 8:15-17, because I am being taxed on something I can't even drive).

This taught me that we can be led astray by our own desires. Like the Israelites, I didn't need a car because there is an excellent transportation system across Europe (1 Samuel 8:7-8). I just wanted one because it seemed everyone else had one (1 Samuel 8:5). In reality, few of my friends owned cars, and they often asked me for rides or to run errands for them all of the time (1 Samuel 8:13).

Another Example: The Wandering Eyes

I had a friend of mine who wanted to be married so bad that she avoided all the signs and warnings God was giving her. Handsome, good bloodline, job, nice car, and all the things a woman looks for in a man; excuse me, I would not know all things women look for. Nevertheless, she wanted to be married, to have someone to hold her at night, and so on (1 Samuel 8:5). God revealed to her his wandering eyes. The Lord warned her, advised her that she would be married but not to him (1 Samuel 8:11-18). God told her and showed her that he was not the one for her by witnessing his wandering eyes before she said, "I do."

A wandering eye, if you don't understand the metaphor, is when a person is looking at and showing interest in another person other than the one they are in a relationship with. I am not talking about the women who catch you off guard walking by gracefully. You glance at them and practice the "bouncing eyes" strategy taught in *Every Man's Battle* by Stephen Arterburn, Fred Stoeker, and Mike Yorkey. They introduced a technique to use when a temptation walks in front of you. You will acknowledge it but bounce your eyes somewhere else. When you practice this, it will become automatic and natural. No, I am talking about the wandering off. Your mind starts thinking of seeking them out, pursuing them, the "I want it all" look. I know you know what I am talking about; whether you are a man or a woman, you know.

Still, she got married. The reason could have been many: she wanted to get out of the parent's house, security, loneliness, in her mind she is getting too old, everybody around her was getting married, or maybe she was a bridesmaid at too many weddings. Who knows the reason she did not listen to the warning? But it happened, she got married, and on the wedding day, he was looking at the bridesmaids, the caterers, the ushers, and probably the preacher. Okay, I went too far, but you know what I'm saying (1 Samuel 8:22). It just got worse. It took another few years before she had to surrender back to what God warned her about in him, and she ended up divorcing.

We do that, don't we? We "mess up" and, instead of admitting that we made a mistake, a bad choice, or an unwise decision, we stay in our mess, smell and all, for way longer than we should stay because we may be ashamed, embarrassed, feeling guilty, or in denial, thinking that he or the situation will change or fix itself. Why would the situation change or fix itself if we knowingly walked into the mess? God would not have warned us first if there was not a reason. He will always direct or redirect us.

The key is one of the first rules of safety we learned growing up: it was to stop, look, and listen to the warnings. When you hear the voices, stop, look at who's talking to you, listen to what is being said. God reveals to you the answer or solution. You must know God's voice. Sometimes there are a lot of voices, including yours. God's voice will never lead you astray. The other voices, most of the time even your own voice, will offer reason: the reason why it is okay to do what is wrong, the reason why doing it anyway is good, and, like a song I know says, "the reason that we're here..." is because we listen to "Reason."

If "Reason" were an actual person, he is the one who never sticks around to see the mess you end up with. He is the one who always hears his momma calling him home when something breaks. You remember that "friend?"

Lessons Learned

When we have studied the Scripture and come to the request line, we will get the same supporting scriptures.

What can be learned from this?

- Listen carefully to God's guidance, especially when you strongly desire something.
- Consider the long-term consequences of the decision.
- Don't compare yourself to others or make decisions based on what "everyone else" is doing.
- Even if God allows you to have something, it doesn't necessarily mean it's His best for you.
- God can turn our mistakes into blessings if we repent and align ourselves with His will.

When We Ask for Life Itself

What happens when we're asking God for life itself, for a child? What do we do when we ask and don't receive? Do we take matters into our own hands? And who will offer honest counsel when everyone around us feels obligated to "touch and agree" simply to show support?

A Story of Patient Faith

I know a couple who exemplifies faithful waiting. After receiving their long-awaited baby boy, they shared their journey of trusting God's timing rather than forcing their own.

For years, they had tried to conceive naturally, choosing prayer over artificial intervention. They believed that if God wanted them to have a child, He would provide one in His timing. During those waiting years, they endured a painful development process, watching "other people" have baby after baby. Brothers, sisters, friends, even those they considered adversaries, seemed to conceive effortlessly.

Everywhere they looked, children appeared, at church, at work, in grocery stores, especially during holidays when family gatherings highlighted their empty arms. Well-meaning friends would ask, "Why don't you have children?" while bouncing their own squirming toddlers.

Then, one day, it happened. They received their miracle. Their story may not be everyone's path, but their focus remained constant: trusting God's timing rather than trying to do His work for Him.

When Control Meets Divine Sovereignty

Consider another couple's contrasting approach. The wife methodically controlled every aspect of her life: remaining single on purpose, single through her prime childbearing years for education and career advancement, accumulating wealth, traveling at will, maintaining complete control over her circumstances.

She found it easy to trust God, but when we examined her heart more closely, a different story emerged. Having achieved everything on her checklist, she now wanted a baby on her timeline to feel like a woman. One fact, and only one obstacle, remained: she could not see that she was already a woman, and God gives life. Despite repeated attempts, no child came.

The couple pursued every medical intervention available: in vitro fertilization (IVF), unsuccessful; intrauterine insemination (IUI), unsuccessful; intracervical insemination (ICI), unsuccessful. They discovered a humbling truth: you cannot control God.

We're often misled by scientific advancement. While medical technology can assist conception, God still has the final word on life. We may want to control everything, but the truth remains: God is sovereign, we are not. There have been cases through science which left couples with way more than they bargained for; four, five, six children at one time. It is nice when we feel in control of a situation, right? Remember this: when we feel in control, we and situations often get out of control.

Like the Israelites, if we want to see God move, we must resist the urge to "help" Him. Consider this question: if those medical procedures had succeeded, who would receive the glory? While glory ultimately belongs to the Giver of life, who would likely take credit? The couple would, feeling they had "won" by achieving their goal through "every means necessary," often ignoring spiritual wisdom and counsel along the way, but they got what they wanted.

Learning to Listen in Silence

When you sense God's silence, listen carefully. Distinguish between His directions, redirections, and delays. These may sound like denials, but they are not. God's instructions are never rejection; they are protection, redirection, or divine timing for our development. Everything centers on His will. Our delays may stem from various causes: lack of obedience, spiritual laziness, inconsistent character, insufficient knowledge, wrong motives, or need for greater experiences. But we can be confident that everything we do through Him will work for our good every time. He will provide for our needs and grant the desires of our hearts according to His perfect timing and methods.

There is wisdom in the wait. Sometimes God's greatest gift is not giving us what we want when we want it but preparing us for what He knows we truly need. In the waiting, we discover whether we're seeking to fulfill His purposes or simply demanding He fulfill ours.

The question isn't whether God hears our prayers, He always does. The question is whether we're willing to trust His answer, even when it requires more faith than we feel ready to give.

Self-Evaluation Questions:

- **Israel's Demand for a King:** In 1 Samuel 8, God warned Israel about the consequences of having a king, but they insisted anyway. How does this story illustrate the difference between God allowing something and God blessing something? Can you think of times when you've insisted on something despite warnings?
- **Personal Desires vs. Godly Wisdom:** The author's story about buying a car in Europe shows how desire can blind

us to practical wisdom. What desires in your life might be clouding your judgment? How can we better distinguish between needs and wants?

- **Warning Signs in Relationships:** The example of the friend who ignored warning signs about her fiancé's «wandering eyes» illustrates how badly wanting something can make us dismiss red flags. How can we maintain objectivity when we desperately want something? What role should trusted counsel play?

- **Trusting God's Timing:** The contrasting stories of couples trying to have children show different approaches to trusting God. What's the difference between faith and taking control? How do we balance medical intervention with trusting God's sovereignty?

- **Learning to Listen in Silence:** The chapter suggests that God's silence isn't rejection but may involve directions, redirections, or delays. How can we better distinguish between these different types of divine responses? What spiritual disciplines help us hear God more clearly during waiting periods?

Moment of Prayer:

I come before You with a humble heart, recognizing my need for Your divine guidance. Protect me from the pitfalls that my own understanding cannot see and grant me the wisdom to discern Your voice above all others, above my emotions, my desires, and even my own reasoning.

Lord, tune my spiritual ears to hear Your truth clearly through Your Word. When my heart pulls me in one direction, help me to pause and seek Your direction first. Give me the patience to wait for Your counsel and the courage to follow it, even when it challenges my natural inclinations. Examine my current concerns and burdens with Your perfect insight. Reveal to me which of my requests align with Your will and which stem from selfish ambition. Transform my desires so they reflect Your heart and bring glory to Your name. Amen.

CHAPTER SEVEN

Parable of the Left, Right, and Back

This story reveals a profound spiritual principle that governs our relationship with our Heavenly Father. When we abandon God's guidance because His timing seems too slow, His methods too indirect, or His path too circuitous, we often find ourselves facing exactly the dangers and difficulties He was lovingly steering us away from. Trust in the Lord's timing and His knowledge of the road ahead. He sees the dangers you cannot see, and His guidance, even when it seems slow, is always working for your ultimate good.

This is a powerful parable about patience, trust, and the dangers of abandoning guidance.

The Parable

A young man asked his father if they could stop at McDonald's on their way home. "Of course," his father replied warmly. As they began their journey, the son's anticipation grew into impatience.

"Are we there yet?" he asked, his hunger mounting.

"We're getting close. Can you see the golden arches?" his father responded calmly.

The young man spotted the familiar sign and began tapping his foot restlessly. "I really need to use the bathroom, Dad."

"I know, son. We're taking this route to avoid the highway traffic," his father explained, continuing to drive through what seemed like an unnecessarily long path.

Along the way, the father pointed out the beauty around them: trees displaying their autumn colors, an immaculate Mercedes S-Class gliding past, a fellow church member entering a local store. He was sharing the journey, trying to connect with his son and teach him to notice life's details.

But the young man had reached his limit. When they stopped at a red light just four blocks from McDonald's, he made a fateful decision. Without warning, he bolted from the car, nearly colliding with oncoming traffic.

"Dad, I'll meet you there!" he shouted, disappearing between two buildings before his father could respond.

"Son, don't go that way!" his father called out, but it was too late. The young man, let's call him Nate, had already vanished into the unknown.

Behind those buildings, Nate stumbled into something he never expected: three gang members conducting illegal business. His sudden appearance interrupted their activities, and the consequences were swift and brutal. Nate found himself in a fight he couldn't win, barely escaping when the distant sound of police sirens scattered his attackers.

But his troubles weren't over. Attempting to continue his shortcut, Nate jumped a fence, only to discover a territorial guard dog waiting on the other side. The animal's powerful jaws clamped down on his ankle before he managed to escape to the opposite side of the property.

Injured and shaken, Nate reached an alley with two choices: he could go left or right. He chose right, seeing it would lead to the main street and finally to McDonald's. Remarkably, he had managed to hold his bladder through the violent encounter with the gang members, but the terrifying dog attack had proven too much; he had soiled himself in fear.

When Nate finally reached the main street, he was only half a block from his destination. And there, waiting at the stoplight just before McDonald's, was his father's car.

His father's face lit up with relief and concern when he saw his son's disheveled, limping figure. "Son, you jumped out so quickly! I couldn't warn you. This is the neighborhood where I grew up. This area isn't safe for running around alone. Are you okay?"

In that moment, Nate realized the painful truth: his father's seemingly slow route wasn't about delays or distractions. It was about protection, wisdom, and safety. His impatience had led him directly into dangers his father had been carefully helping him avoid.

The Spiritual Truth

This story explains a profound spiritual truth: when we abandon God's guidance because His timing seems too slow or His path too indirect, we often find ourselves facing dangers and difficulties He was lovingly steering us away from. Sometimes what feels like delay is actually divine protection, and what appears to be the longest route is truly the safest path.

Remember, staying focused on God's plan for you, rather than looking left and right at what others have, is crucial. You don't know the full story behind others' possessions or achievements. Trust in God's wisdom and guidance, and you'll find true fulfillment and purpose.

Self-Evaluation Questions:

- **Impatience and Consequences:** In the parable, Nate's impatience led him into dangerous situations his father was helping him avoid. Reflect on times when your impatience caused you to abandon wise guidance. What were the consequences, and what did you learn?
- **Divine Protection Through Apparent Delays:** The father's «slow» route was actually protective, not punitive. How might some of God's apparent delays in your life actually be forms of protection? What situations can you now see differently in this light?
- **The Danger of Shortcuts:** Nate chose what seemed like a shortcut but encountered gang members and a guard dog. What spiritual or life «shortcuts» are tempting but potentially dangerous? How can we learn to trust the longer, safer path God provides?
- **Trust vs. Control:** The story illustrates the difference between trusting guidance and taking control. In what areas of your life do you struggle most with wanting to take control rather than following God's lead?
- **Looking Left and Right:** The chapter ends with advice about not looking at what others have but staying focused

on God's plan for you. How does comparison with others derail us from God's best? What practical steps can help us maintain focus on our own journey?

Moment of Prayer:

May I trust not in my own understanding, but acknowledge You in all my ways, knowing that You will direct my paths. Keep me on the narrow road that leads to life, away from the broad path of compromise and error. In the mighty name of Jesus, who is the Way, the Truth, and the Life, I pray. Amen.

Memorize:

"Trust in the Lord with all your heart and lean not on your own understanding; in all your ways acknowledge Him, and He shall direct your paths." Proverbs 3:5-6, NKJV

CHAPTER EIGHT

Discovering the Will of God

This theological chapter explores the relationship between God's sovereignty and human free will, drawing on Augustine's four types of will: created (like a hinge allowing choice), fallen (bound by sin), redeemed (rooted in love), and fully free (perfected in eternity). The chapter discusses discerning God's will through renewed minds (Romans 12:2, KJV) and distinguishes between God's hidden and revealed will using examples of Abraham, Moses, and Israel's kingship. It emphasizes submitting to God's will as Jesus did, using Daniel's friends' bold faith as an example. The chapter concludes with understanding prayer in Jesus' name and overcoming doubts about prayer's effectiveness.

The Concept of God's Will

The concept of the will of God requires an investigation of several practical aspects. We have discussed the nature of God, its implications for our freedom, and how we, as believers, can discern and align our requests with God's intentions.

Free Will and Divine Sovereignty

The nature of God's sovereignty coexists with the freedom of choice that every human has when they decide to obey or disobey advice. That is your choice, called free will. If someone were to warn you not to go into a burning building, and you go in anyway, there is a 100% catastrophic consequence in the decision that you made. We have read or heard about thrill-seekers ignoring the "DO NOT ENTER!" or "STAY BEHIND THIS LINE!" signs and warnings; for instance, staying off the edge of Niagara Falls, and some still disobeyed the warnings with deadly consequences.

We really do not have to do anything in this world but die. We don't even have to pay taxes (I am not suggesting that). But we must all die one day, maybe not today, but one day. It is the choices that we make that will determine our eternal destination. If we have no choice, there is no free will. If we do not have a choice to do right or wrong, go left or right, stay or go, lead, follow, or walk with, then is it free will? I believe not.

In the last chapter, I introduced the parable of "Nate, the impatient one." He could have stayed in the car and avoided a world of hurt and discomfort. He had a choice to stay in the car with his father or get out at any time. He exited the vehicle and entered unknown, unforeseen circumstances. Just think, if he had asked his father if it would be okay to walk to McDonald's, taking the shortcut, the insight his father could have informed him about various times he tried, reminding him it is not safe. Maybe Nate would have gone anyway but being vigilant. Still, after vigilance, he would have ended up at the same spot: do you go left or right? When he got to the main street again, he found his father there, scratching his head, wondering why go through the trouble of running or walking when I am already taking you there.

Theological Perspectives on Free Will

St. Augustine identifies four types of human will:

1. **The created will, which he describes as a hinge:** This is the original will that was given to humans by God at creation. Like a hinge, it allows for movement and choice. For example, Adam and Eve in the Garden of Eden had the ability to choose whether to obey God or eat the forbidden fruit.
2. **The fallen will, a link in a chain binding human beings to sin:** This is the will affected by original sin. For instance, a person might know that lying is wrong but still choose to lie to avoid consequences, illustrating how our will is bound to sinful tendencies.
3. **The redeemed will, which is a root of love:** This is the will of a person who has accepted Christ and is being transformed by God's grace. An example would be someone who, out of love for God and others, chooses to forgive those who have wronged them, even when it's difficult.
4. **The fully free will, to be enjoyed in the next life, when perfection is made complete:** This is the will we will have in heaven, completely aligned with God's will and free from the influence of sin. While we can't experience this fully on earth, moments of perfect peace and alignment with God's will give us a glimpse of what this might be like.

These four types of will show the progression of human nature; from creation, through the fall, to redemption, and finally to glorification in eternal life.

Discerning God's Will

Discerning and aligning our requests with God's intentions is a result of a renewed mind. Romans 12:2 instructs us that we should not be conformed to this world but be transformed by the renewing of our mind. We need to renew our minds. We must learn the things of God and the ways of Jesus. Then you will be able to test and approve what is the good, pleasing, and perfect will of God for your life.

Hidden and Revealed Will of God

Thomas Aquinas and some contemporary theologians believe there is God's hidden will and His revealed will. Abraham's call, Moses leading the Israelites, and the kingship of Israel are reflections of the will of God being revealed and challenged. We see these aspects of God's will played out in several biblical narratives:

Abraham's call: God revealed His will for Abraham to leave his homeland (Genesis 12:1–3, KJV), but the full scope of God's plan, to create a nation that would bless the world, was hidden at the time.

Moses leading the Israelites: God's revealed will was for Moses to lead the people out of Egypt, but the challenges they would face and the forty years in the wilderness were part of God's hidden will, gradually unveiled.

The kingship of Israel: God's revealed will was initially for Israel to be a theocracy, with Him as their King. However, when the people demanded a human king, God's hidden will allowed for this, using it to eventually bring about the lineage of David, leading to Jesus.

These examples show how God's revealed will often interacts with human choices and circumstances, while His hidden will continues to work behind the scenes. They also illustrate how God's will can be both revealed and challenged, as humans grapple with obedience and understanding.

Understanding this distinction can help us trust God even when we don't understand His ways. We can focus on obeying His revealed will while trusting that His hidden will is working all things together for good (Romans 8:28, KJV).

Submitting to God's Will

Allowing God's will to be done, as Jesus prayed in Matthew 6:10 and in the Garden of Gethsemane, as Matthew 26:39 reads, *"but not my will, but let your will be done,"* makes us available to God's grace and blessings. There is something we must learn about this statement *"...but let your will be done."* It is that when we make this statement, we must believe that God has our best interest in mind and accept that the will of God is the best for us.

There are many examples of submitting to God's will. You could probably think of some in your life or the life of someone you know. I can think of a few now: my father, who I believe followed the will of God through the urban renewal project which helped to shape Olathe, Kansas; Charles Harrison Mason, who through the leading of the Lord, started the Church of God in Christ; Dr. Martin Luther King Jr., who needs no introduction; and many others you may know.

There are some biblical examples of believers who submitted to the will of God and, through trust in Him, paved the way for us all, spiritually and naturally.

Biblical Example: Faith in God's Will

In the second and third chapters of Daniel, we find a powerful example of faith in God's will. Daniel had become a ruler over the whole province of Babylon after he interpreted King Nebuchadnezzar's dream. Daniel made his fellows, Shadrach, Meshach, and Abednego, overseers of the province of Babylon. After the king erected an image of gold, he wanted everyone to bow to it. Daniel's fellows did not bow to the king's image. Their statement to him is something we need to investigate.

Shadrach, Meshach, and Abednego spoke boldly, refusing to bow to Nebuchadnezzar, saying, *"We are not careful to answer thee in this matter. If it be so, our God whom we serve is able to deliver us from the burning fiery furnace, and he will deliver us out of thine hand, O king. But if not, be it known unto thee, O king, that we will not serve thy gods, nor worship the golden image which thou hast set up"* (Daniel 3:16–18, KJV).

Overcoming Doubts in Prayer

Another attack of Satan may be to cause you to doubt the effectiveness of prayer. He may whisper to you, "You don't think God is personally interested in you? He's far away and concerned about more important things. Surely you don't think He'll hear your prayers, much less answer them!"

But with Jesus Christ as your Savior and Lord, you have the unique privilege of speaking directly with your heavenly Father through Him. God wants you to come confidently into His presence through Christ and to talk to Him about everything (look up Philippians 4:6 and Hebrews 4:14-16, KJV). He is intensely interested in you and your needs.

The Power of Praying in Jesus' Name

In John 16:24 (KJV), Jesus was speaking to His disciples the night before His crucifixion. He did not tell them they had never asked for anything in prayer; He said they had not asked anything in Jesus' name. You have probably prayed many times, especially when in trouble. As a believer in Christ, you can ask in Jesus' name because you belong to Him. To ask in His name means to ask in His authority and on His merit. Just as the Father answered Jesus' every prayer, He will answer you when you ask in Jesus' name, that God may get the glory.

We will illuminate the glory of God in the next chapter to understand "to the glory of God." As we continue to discover God's will, remember that it may involve challenges and triumphs during the process. My father on the urban renewal project had challenges during a time when a railroad track divided one community from the next. C.H. Mason was challenged, but his leading built a temple during a time when it was difficult for an African American to build. Dr. King faced many challenges during his leadership toward human equality, and Daniel and many others in the Bible stood on the will of God, which ultimately led to victory and fulfillment in our spiritual and natural lives.

Self-Evaluation Questions:

- **Free Will and Divine Sovereignty:** The chapter discusses how God's sovereignty coexists with human free will, using Augustine's four types of will. How do you understand the balance between God's control and human choice? Which of Augustine's categories best describes your current spiritual state?

- **Hidden vs. Revealed Will:** The concept that God has both hidden and revealed will is illustrated through biblical examples like Abraham and Moses. How does understanding this distinction help when we don't understand God's ways? What is God's clearly revealed will that we can always obey?
- **Renewed Mind and Discernment:** Romans 12:2 speaks of being *"transformed by the renewing of your mind"* to discern God's will. What does it mean practically to renew your mind? How has studying God's Word changed your ability to recognize His guidance?
- **Submitting to God's Will:** Like Jesus in Gethsemane saying, *"not my will, but yours,"* true prayer involves submission. What's the difference between asking God to bless our plans versus asking to be part of His plans? In what areas do you struggle the most with submission?
- **Faith in Uncertain Outcomes:** Shadrach, Meshach, and Abednego said God could deliver them *"but if not"* they still wouldn't bow to the idol. How does this kind of faith, trusting God regardless of outcomes, relate to receiving His "Yes"? What would this look like in your current circumstances?

Moment of Prayer:

God, when You speak to me, I will listen and trust that You have my best interest in mind. Amen.

CHAPTER NINE

Discovering the Will of God: "The Focus Is Not on You"

Building on the Lord's Prayer, this chapter emphasizes that true prayer focuses on God's glory rather than personal desires. It examines Jesus' promise in John 14:12-14 about doing *"greater things,"* explaining this refers not just to miracles but to spreading God's Word globally. Using the example of a conference "Yes Desk," the chapter illustrates how accommodation works when it serves the greater good, not personal glory. The *"greater things"* believers can do include worldwide evangelism and demonstrating God's love. The key principle is that requests aligned with God's will and bringing Him glory receive affirmative responses.

When we were younger, many of us learned the "Lord's Prayer." In Matthew 6:9-13 (KJV), Jesus teaches:

> *"Our Father in heaven, hallowed be your name. Your kingdom come, your will be done, on earth as it is in heaven. Give us this day our daily bread, and forgive us our trespasses, as we also have forgiven those who trespass*

against us. And lead us not into temptation but deliver us from evil."

I vividly remember learning this prayer during vacation Bible school in 4th grade. Along with memorizing the books of the Bible and the 23rd Psalm, mastering the Lord's Prayer felt like a significant achievement. The concluding line, "For yours is the kingdom and the power and the glory forever. Amen," emphasizes a crucial point: in all our asking, God must receive the glory.

This focus on God's glory is essential when considering His will and our prayers. God loves us deeply, but He's not a genie in a bottle granting wishes at our every whim. Our relationship with Him is far more profound and purposeful.

Understanding the Lord's Prayer

One of the most discussed verses among my fellow Christians is John 14:14 (KJV). To understand its context, let's look at the passage beginning from verse 9. Jesus, addressing His disciples' requests to see God, explains that seeing Him is equivalent to seeing the Father. He emphasizes that His works are not His own, but the Father working through Him.

Then Jesus makes a remarkable statement:

"Very truly I tell you, whoever believes in me will do the works I have been doing, and they will do even greater things than these, because I am going to the Father. And I will do whatever you ask in my name, so that the Father may be glorified in the Son. You may ask me for anything in my name, and I will do it" (John 14:12-14, NIV).

This passage continues to reinforce my conviction that God does not say "No" when we are truly aligned with His will. However, this statement requires careful interpretation and spiritual maturity. It's not a blank check for our selfish desires, a "blab it and grab it," or "name it and claim it" guarantee, but rather a profound promise rooted in surrendering our will to God's purposes and seeking His glory above all else.

Aligning Our Requests with God's Will

To illustrate this concept, let me share a personal experience that profoundly impacted my understanding of God's willingness to say "yes."

At a conference in Florida, I encountered what they called the "Yes Desk," a customer service station with an extraordinary philosophy. Their commitment was simple yet powerful: solving every attendee's problem with a "yes," no matter how challenging it might seem.

I found myself facing what appeared to be an impossible situation. I needed lodging but had no room reservation at the conference hotel, and I was told that the hotel was completely booked. When I approached the Yes Desk with my dilemma, I honestly expected them to apologize and keep me at the offsite hotel down the street from the conference.

Instead, they immediately sprang into action with remarkable determination. Despite the apparent impossibility of the situation, they worked tirelessly to find a creative solution. To my amazement, ten minutes later, they had secured me a room in the very conference hotel where I had hoped to stay. What seemed impossible became reality through their commitment to saying "yes."

This experience sparked a profound reflection: If human beings, with all their limitations, can demonstrate such dedication to meeting needs and solving problems, how much greater is our Heavenly Father's desire and ability to provide what we truly need?

However, this revelation also taught me an important lesson about motives and alignment with purpose. For instance, if I had approached that Yes Desk with a self-serving request, say, demanding they arrange for a luxury limousine to pick me up at the airport, that request would have been focused entirely on elevating my personal status rather than serving the conference's mission or my genuine needs.

Now they, based on their reputation, could have arranged such transportation, but it would have come at a significant personal cost, far more than I would have wanted to pay. The service would have shifted from meeting a legitimate need to indulging personal vanity.

This principle applies powerfully to our relationship with God. When we ask Him for things that fall outside His perfect will for our lives; requests motivated by pride, selfishness, or a desire for personal glory, He may indeed allow us to have what we're demanding. But we must understand that receiving things outside His will always comes at a price that's ultimately higher than we want to pay.

The cost might be measured in money we can't afford to lose, time we desperately need for more important purposes, or commitments that drain our energy from what truly matters. More importantly, pursuing desires outside God's will costs us peace, joy, relationships, and spiritual growth.

The "Yes Desk" taught me that the most satisfying "yes" comes when our requests align with the greater purpose and mission we're part of, whether that's a conference's objectives or, more importantly, God's perfect plan for our lives.

The Concept of "Greater Things"

When we align ourselves with His will, God directs our steps in remarkable ways, just as Scripture promises. Let me share two powerful examples from my time working as an undercover investigator that demonstrate this *"and they will do even greater things than these"* divine guidance.

The Gas Station Robbery

I was working as a drug investigator who also assisted with general crimes when a gas station robbery occurred. The case seemed impossible. There was virtually no evidence, no witnesses, and no clear leads pointing to any suspect. The investigation had reached a dead end. In that moment of uncertainty, I turned to prayer, asking the Lord to direct me to whoever had committed this crime.

A few hours later, I was led to visit the gas station. As I walked in, I noticed one of the employees, and the Spirit of God immediately identified him to me as the perpetrator. Without revealing my identity as an investigator, I approached him calmly and said, "I know what you did. You're going to need to call us at 9:00 am and tell us everything. There's serious trouble coming if you don't." He asked who I was, and I walked out. I went back to the office, where I informed my colleague that the perp would be calling at 9:00 am that morning.

At exactly 9:00 am, he called and confessed to not only the gas station robbery but identified his accomplice. God's guidance had led me directly to the answer when human investigation had failed.

The Vehicle Lot Vandalism

This case was even more challenging. Someone had caused $37,000 worth of damage to a vehicle storage lot, destroying windshield wipers and side-view mirrors on multiple cars. The only evidence was a single footprint with a distinctive "FILA" shoe brand pattern on the bottom of it.

The Agent in Charge informed me that solving this high-profile case would require me to work through the weekend if we didn't solve it, meaning I wouldn't be able to attend church services. This troubled me deeply because worship and fellowship were priorities in my life. I prayed sincerely, asking the Lord to help me identify the criminal quickly so I could still honor my commitment to worship.

The next morning, I felt led to go to a bus stop. As I stood there, I simply looked down and began observing people's feet. Suddenly, I spotted someone wearing FILA shoes with the exact pattern we were looking for. When I looked up at the young man wearing them, our eyes met, and I could see immediate guilt written across his face.

"Come here," I said, and began asking him questions. Without any coercion or pressure, he confessed to the vandalism and implicated his friend as well. He was so relieved to finally tell the truth. His father was incredibly grateful for how respectfully I had handled the situation with his son, thanking me for treating the young man with dignity even while holding him accountable for his actions.

Later, the recognition and the real glory came when I shared with everyone the true source of my success in these high-profile cases. I received an award from the Commander of the Military Installation, where he specifically mentioned my "unique investigative skills." While I accepted the recognition graciously, it was divine guidance, not human cleverness, that had led to these breakthroughs.

This is where God receives the glory, even when others can't see His hand at work. When we genuinely seek to do God's will and ask for His assistance in serving others and seeking justice, He is faithful to provide direction and wisdom beyond our natural abilities.

These experiences taught me that when we pray according to God's will; seeking justice, truth, and the good of others rather than personal gain, He responds in ways that can only be described as miraculous. The key is to ensure that our requests align with His purposes and that we remain humble about the source of our success, giving Him the glory He deserves.

Not a Fairy Tale

I share these experiences not as fairy tales, but as authentic testimony to how God orchestrates the details of our lives when we align our hearts with His purposes.

My desire was simple: to re-enlist in the military. I had concluded my first career at 14 years of service, but a few years later felt called to return. What unfolded next reveals the intricate way God weaves our longings into His greater design.

To fully appreciate this story, I must begin with an earlier desire, our dream to be stationed in Hawaii. During my previous service, I was scheduled for a military transfer from

Germany to somewhere in the United States. The orders came through: New Mexico, followed by Korea. Not Hawaii, but the dream persisted quietly in our hearts.

The timing of this next statement is nothing short of God-directed. When I submitted my re-enlistment application, something happened to my paperwork, a delay that initially seemed frustrating. When I called to check the status, I was told to resubmit everything. Instead of becoming angry, I simply complied with what the personnel office requested. The representative assisting me asked a routine question: "Where would you like to be stationed?"

"Hawaii?" I responded, more hopeful than expectant.

"Interesting," he replied. "A position just opened up that you could slide right into."

As I prayed about this unexpected opportunity, the Lord said something remarkable into my spirit: "You will be pastoring in Hawaii." When I shared this with my wife, her response amazed me: "Okay!" No questions, no hesitation; just peaceful acceptance.

Not only did we receive the pastoral calling, but we also received something we did not anticipate, a fifth child. Not through natural conception, but through foster care that led to adoption. This addition was particularly significant because we had previously decided not to have any more children after age 30, wanting our youngest of four to be out of the house two years before I turned 50. "Our plan," was so perfect in our eyes that only God could change plans we had set so firmly in stone, with a chisel of confidence.

Our ministry calling flourished beyond what I had envisioned. I served as pastor of First Paradise Christian Fellowship Church of God in Christ, and shortly after, Hilo Prayer Center Church of God in Christ. Each assignment brought unique opportunities to serve God's people and witness His faithfulness. As we continue discovering God's will for our lives, we must remember this essential truth: while He delights in blessing us, the ultimate focus remains not on our wants but on His glory and the fulfillment of His perfect plan through every believer.

Our role is simply to trust and watch as His glorious blessings overtake us on the journey. When our desires align with His will, we discover that God's provision exceeds our imagination, not just meeting our needs but positioning us for purposes we never could have orchestrated ourselves.

The Hawaii dream that began as a simple desire for a beautiful duty station became the backdrop for pastoral ministry, family expansion, and spiritual growth that continues to impact lives today. This is how God works, taking our humble requests and transforming them into platforms for His kingdom purposes.

Self-Evaluation Questions:

- **The Lord's Prayer and Glory:** The Lord's Prayer emphasizes *"Yours is the kingdom and the power and the glory forever."* How does keeping God's glory as the focus change the way we pray? What requests have you made that were more about your glory than His?

- **The "Yes Desk" Principle:** The conference Yes Desk story illustrates serving a greater purpose versus personal comfort. How can we discern when our requests are aligned with God's mission versus our own agenda? What's an example from your life?
- **Greater Things Through Alignment:** The investigative stories show how God provided supernatural guidance when the focus was on justice and service. When have you experienced God's direction in ways that brought Him glory? How did alignment with His will change the outcome?
- **Cost of Misaligned Requests:** The chapter warns that getting what we want outside God's will comes at a higher price than we want to pay. Have you experienced this? What did it cost you to pursue something God wasn't blessing?
- **Hawaii Story Application:** The author's re-enlistment and Hawaii assignment came with divine confirmation and purpose beyond his expectations. How does this story challenge you to trust God's orchestration of your desires? What dreams are you holding that need to be surrendered to His larger purpose?

A Moment of Prayer:

God, when You speak to me, I will listen and trust that You have my best interest in mind. Amen.

CHAPTER TEN

God Says "Yes": The "Every Time" of God

This practical chapter challenges us to examine our motives when we believe God has said "No." Through a one-minute exercise, you will reflect on times we felt rejected by God, then analyze whether our requests were according to His will and for His glory. I share powerful testimonies, including a miraculous provision of fuel in Germany that brought glory to God. The chapter addresses sensitive topics like praying for healing versus death, emphasizing that God receives glory in all circumstances. It corrects misunderstandings about popular verses like 1 John 1:9 and Psalm 37:4, showing how clean hearts and delight in God lead to fulfilled desires.

Examining Our Motives

We are going to bring together everything that we have explored in this book and examine our life. When you asked according to His will, and He was going to be glorified, did He say no? Okay, I get it, you replied, "Yes, he said no!" no to a new car; no to the house you wanted; no to the job; no to the healing; no to marrying that man; no to marrying that woman; to having children; and no to whatever I did not mention.

Here is an exercise for you. For the next minute, I want you to think of a time that you believe God told you no. Really, do it. Take a minute. I will wait, and like God said to Job in chapter 38, *"you will listen!"*

ONE MINUTE PRACTICAL EXERCISE

Think about the time when you felt that God told you no. Was there anything else that He said, or was it just a flat-out no? When God answered in the Bible, did He just say no, or did God give us an explanation for why we should or should not have done a thing, or why we didn't need a thing? Were there instructions? Were you ready for the yes?

Paul pleaded with God in 2 Corinthians 12:7-9 (NIV) to take away a thorn in his flesh, a messenger of Satan, to torment him. He asked three times to take it away from him, and He said, *"My grace is sufficient for you, for my power is made perfect in weakness."*

Finally, was your request according to God's will? When Jesus spoke to the disciples and told them that they could do more than He had done, he was not referring to material things only. If that natural thing will give God glory, it's a yes!

Personal Testimonies of God's Yes

I was in Germany in Europe. If you have ever driven in Germany, you will remember the highway called the autobahn. The highway was an experience I had never had. If you want to get off the autobahn, you use the exit ramp. If you did not, you would not have any exit for 20 to 30 miles up the road.

I missed my turn. When I got back on track, my gas was low. Another thing about the highway is that the fueling points were not like the United States, every 10 to 30 miles in most cases. I was on my way back from a church district meeting, and my gas gauge read "E." You know, empty. I know my car; you, like you know your car, and how long you can drive on E. I was worried because I was at the "EFR" level of E. That is the *empty for real* level.

What I did was place a small piece of paper over the gas gauge to take my focus off the problem and went to God. I made it to the gas station and took the paper off of the gauge, and you know what? The gauge had a quarter of a tank of gas in it. I had not even put gas in it yet. I did not keep it a secret; I told everybody what God had done, and He would get the glory.

It can be a time of provision that we thought small or something complex. When God supposedly told you no, was He going to get the glory, or were you? Were you praying a selfish or self-centered prayer? God will get the glory even in sickness or the death of a loved one. This can be a touchy subject, but I believe we must hear it.

Understanding God's Responses

An example of the glory in death would be if a son's father is on his deathbed and the son prays to God, for instance, "Don't let my father die," and the son's intention is that the son he understandably wants his father around longer. Because his request is for his comfort, he must remember to say, "But Lord, not my will be done, but Your will be done, that You may get the glory."

It is not the life of the son, and he really does not know what his father is asking God to do for him. Some of the thoroughbreds have argued, "Where is the glory in that? His father is gone." Play out the events following his father's death. The father's death may have caused the son to step up and have a closer relationship with God, or maybe it drew him and his family closer, or separated the family for a time to show them things they had to deal with. I don't know your truth, but you do. Search the truth and stop blaming God when you ask out of His will and can't get what you want.

A friend of mine called me to ask for prayer. I prayed with them about their sick parent. After we prayed, I hung up the phone and prayed again because, for a moment, I thought, *What if my prayer for healing ended up with a dead parent?* Be about your Father's business, and you will always get a yes.

The Lord showed me that the parent's healing in this situation would build the faith of the friend and give Him the glory; build the faith of my young friend concerning that parent. I almost doubted my prayer because I didn't know my friend's mother or her name, or how long she was sick, or really understand what sickness was attacking her body. All I knew was this friend of mine needed God to do something about the situation and called me, and we prayed together.

I was able to petition the Lord on the outcome. He let me know that she would make it through the surgery she needed. There will be times when we don't know what to pray. Nonetheless, God will always get the glory, in life or in death.

The Importance of a Clean Heart

When I was in the world, before I was a believer of God, I thought in my own eyes I was a follower of Christ, but my life did not reflect it. I was doing what I thought I was big enough to do. I was taught whatever I need, God will do it. I just had a distorted understanding of needs. I understood that I could ask God for something, and He would give it to me; "blab it and grab it" prayer. That was so far from accurate.

I would ask for things out of desire for myself. If we could "tell" God what we want, He is "faithful and just" to give it to us. Wrong! Let's get that scripture and read it first to see what it really says. 1 John 1:9 (KJV) reads, *"If we confess our sins, he is faithful and just to forgive us our sins, and to cleanse us from all unrighteousness."*

That scripture has nothing to do with asking for everything you want. It is all about forgiveness of our sins; a clean heart.

Another little something we say is, "Ask God anything, and He will give you the desires of your heart." Here is a question to answer: is your heart a clean heart or a sinful heart? What does that scripture mean? Is that what the scripture really says?

The verse is found in Psalms 51:1–12 (KJV). David has come to the Lord asking God to:

> *"Have mercy upon me, O God, according to thy lovingkindness: according unto the multitude of thy tender mercies blot out my transgressions. Wash me thoroughly from mine iniquity, and cleanse me from my sin. For I acknowledge my transgressions: and my sin is ever before me. Against thee, thee only, have I sinned, and done this evil in thy sight: that thou mightest be justified when thou speakest, and be clear when thou judgest. Behold, I was shapen in iniquity; and in sin did my mother con-*

ceive me. Behold, thou desirest truth in the inward parts: and in the hidden part thou shalt make me to know wisdom. Purge me with hyssop, and I shall be clean: wash me, and I shall be whiter than snow. Make me to hear joy and gladness; that the bones which thou hast broken may rejoice. Hide thy face from my sins and blot out all mine iniquities. Create in me a clean heart, O God; and renew a right spirit within me. Cast me not away from thy presence; and take not thy holy spirit from me. Restore unto me the joy of thy salvation; and uphold me with thy free spirit. Then will I teach transgressors thy ways; and sinners shall be converted unto thee. Deliver me from bloodguiltiness, O God, thou God of my salvation: and my tongue shall sing aloud of thy righteousness. O Lord, open thou my lips; and my mouth shall shew forth thy praise."

Seeking First God's Kingdom

I thought it read that God will give me the desires of my heart. That meant that I don't need to ask, just seek Him first and all His righteousness. Matthew 6:33 (KJV), *"But seek ye first the kingdom of God, and his righteousness; and all these things shall be added unto you."* Psalm 37:4 (KJV), *"Delight thyself also in the Lord: and he shall give thee the desires of thine heart."*

This scenario illustrates the profound challenge of hearing and following God's direction when our deepest longings are at stake. It's particularly difficult because it tests our faith at its core, and without wise counsel, we risk following the crowd instead of God's voice; much like the Israelites who demanded a king when God intended to be their ruler.

The most perilous aspect of these situations is our tendency to surround ourselves with echo-chamber crowds; only the people who "touch and agree" with our desires. Modern church culture often teaches us to avoid anyone who doesn't affirm our wishes and requests, but this leaves us spiritually vulnerable. Like the Israelites, we may unanimously want something that isn't God's best for us, with no one brave enough to offer contrary counsel. Worse still, we often dismiss anyone who dares speak against what we want to hear.

As discussed in Chapter 6, learning to wait on God's timing, especially in matters as sacred as wanting children, requires faith that trusts His sovereignty over our desires for control. The question remains: will we align ourselves with God's will and timing, or will we take matters into our own hands?

Living in the "Yes"

Now we have examined our motives:

1. When we pray, we must ask ourselves if our requests are truly for God's glory or our own comfort and desires.
2. God's responses are detailed: rather than "no" answers, God often provides explanations, instructions, or redirections.
3. Aligning with God's will: true prayer is about seeking God's will and His glory, not manipulating circumstances to fit our desires.
4. God's glory in all circumstances: even in situations we perceive as negative, such as illness or loss, God can be glorified and work for our good.

5. The importance of a clean heart: as we saw in David's prayer, our focus should be on maintaining a pure heart and right relationship with God rather than on material desires.
6. Seeking first God's kingdom: when we prioritize God's kingdom and righteousness, our needs and the desires He places in our hearts will be fulfilled.

Remember, the "Yes" of God is not always what we expect or initially desire. It's "Yes" to His perfect plan, His glory, and our ultimate good. As we move forward in our faith journey, let's strive to align our hearts with God's will, trusting that His "Yes," even when it looks different from what we anticipated, is always the best answer.

By shifting our focus from our wants to God's glory, from our limited perspective to His eternal wisdom, we open ourselves to experience the fullness of God's "Yes" in our lives. Let this understanding transform not only how we pray but how we live, always seeking to glorify God in all circumstances.

As we conclude this exploration of God's affirmative responses, my wife and I are excited to share a personal testimony that vividly illustrates the principles we've discussed. The upcoming bonus chapter features an excerpt from a book my wife and I co-authored and are releasing shortly, detailing our journey to 25 years of marriage.

This intimate account focuses on the first 90 days of our relationship, a period that profoundly demonstrates God's "Yes" and His perfect plan when we attune ourselves to His guidance. Our story serves as a living example of how aligning with God's will, can shape not just our prayers, but our entire lives.

We believe this testimony will not only engage you but also provide practical insights into recognizing and embracing God's affirmative guidance in your own life. It's our hope that through our experiences, you'll gain a deeper understanding of how God's "Yes" can manifest in unexpected and beautiful ways, especially when we're willing to listen and obey.

As you read, we encourage you to reflect on your own journey and consider how God's perfect plan might be unfolding in your life, even in ways you may not yet recognize. Let our story inspire you to trust in God's "Yes," even when the path ahead seems uncertain.

Self-Evaluation Questions:

- **Examining Our Motives:** The chapter challenges us to examine our motives when we believe God said «No.» Think of a specific time when you felt God denied your request. Upon reflection, what was your true motive? Was God going to receive glory from your request?
- **God's Provision and Glory:** My story about my gas gauge miraculously showing a quarter tank illustrates divine provision that brings glory to God. Can you recall times when God provided in ways that clearly pointed to His power? How did you respond?
- **Prayer for Others vs. Self:** The discussion about praying for a dying parent highlights the complexity of prayer motives. How do we pray for others when our emotions are involved? What's the difference between praying for our comfort versus God's will?

- **Scriptural Misunderstanding:** This chapter corrects misinterpretations of verses like 1 John 1:9 and Psalm 37:4. What scriptures have you potentially misunderstood or taken out of context? How does proper biblical interpretation affect our prayer life?
- **Control vs. Trust:** When is medical intervention appropriate, and when does it become an attempt to control God? How do we know when we're helping versus hindering God's plan?

Moment of Prayer:

Search my heart and reveal the true motives behind my prayers. When I feel You have denied my requests, help me honestly examine whether I was seeking my glory or Yours. Forgive me for the times I've approached You with selfish ambitions disguised as spiritual requests.

Thank You for Your miraculous provisions that clearly display Your power and love. Help me to always respond with grateful testimony that points others to You, giving You all the glory for every blessing. In Jesus' name, Amen.

Memorize:

"Search me, O God, and know my heart; test me and know my anxious thoughts. See if there is any offensive way in me and lead me in the way everlasting." - Psalm 139:23-24 (KJV)

CHAPTER ELEVEN

Living in God's "Yes"

As we conclude this journey of discovering God's affirmative nature, let's reflect on what we've learned and how these truths can transform our daily walk with Christ.

The Foundation We've Built

Throughout this book, we've explored a revolutionary understanding of God's responses to our prayers. We've seen that:

- God's fundamental nature is affirmative; all His promises are "Yes" and "Amen" (2 Corinthians 1:20, KJV).
- What we often interpret as "No" is actually guidance, redirection, or preparation.
- Our relationship with God is built on His unchanging character: love, light, holiness, and grace.
- Following God's specific instructions leads to blessing, while deviation leads to consequences.
- Jesus is the perfect example of submitting to God's will while maintaining confidence in the Father's goodness.

- Our motives matter significantly when we approach God with requests.
- God receives glory when we align our desires with His will.

The Practical Application

Now the question becomes: how do we live in the reality of God's "Yes"?

1. Cultivate a Clean Heart

David's prayer in Psalm 51 reminds us that God desires truth in our inner being. Before we present our requests to God, we must examine our hearts:

- Are we harboring unforgiveness?
- Do we have unconfessed sin creating barriers?
- Are our motives pure, seeking God's glory rather than our own?

A clean heart positions us to hear God's voice clearly and receive His affirmative responses.

2. Seek First His Kingdom

Jesus' instruction in Matthew 6:33 isn't simply good advice, it's the key to receiving everything we need. When we prioritize:

- God's glory over our comfort
- His purposes over our plans
- His timing over our urgency
- His methods over our preferences

We find that His "Yes" encompasses far more than we could ask or imagine.

3. Learn to Discern God's Voice

Throughout this book, we've seen examples of people who heard God's direction and those who didn't. The difference often came down to:

- Regular time in God's Word
- A consistent prayer life
- Spiritual community and accountability
- Willingness to obey even when it's difficult
- Patience to wait for confirmation

4. Trust the Process

Remember the parable of the young man who jumped out of his father's car? Impatience caused him to encounter dangers his father was steering him away from. God's delays are not denials; they're often divine protection or preparation for something greater.

5. Give God the Glory

The true test of whether we're operating in God's will is simple: will God receive glory from the outcome? When our prayers, plans, and pursuits bring honor to God's name, we can be confident we're moving in His "Yes."

Your Next Steps

As you close this book, I encourage you to:

Reflect: Look back over your life and identify times you thought God said «No.» Can you now see them as redirections, preparations, or instances where your requests weren't aligned with His will?

Repent: If you've blamed God for unanswered prayers when the real issue was your motives or timing, take time to repent and realign your heart with His purposes.

Rejoice: Celebrate the times God has clearly said «Yes» to you, not just in giving you what you wanted, but in giving you what you needed.

Request: Approach God with new confidence, knowing that when you ask according to His will, for His glory, His response is affirmative. But also approach Him with humility, willing to hear His instructions and follow His redirection.

Remember: God is not a cosmic vending machine or a genie in a bottle. He's your loving Father who knows what you need before you ask, who works all things together for your good, and whose plans for you are always better than your own.

A Final Word

My wife and I have lived the truth of God's "Yes" for over three decades. From our miraculous meeting to our return to Germany, from pastoral ministry in Hawaii to the writing of this book, God has proven faithful to every word He spoke. The same God who orchestrated our story is orchestrating yours.

The question isn't whether God will say "Yes" to you, it's whether you'll align yourself with His will so you can receive and recognize His affirmative response.

As you step forward from here, remember:

- God loves you deeply.
- God hears every prayer.
- God is working in your life right now.

- God's "Yes" is already in motion when you walk in His will.
- God receives glory when you trust Him completely.

Your story of God's "Yes" is being written right now. Walk in faith, trust in His timing, and watch Him fulfill every promise He's made to you.

Self-Evaluation Questions:

- **Transformation Assessment:** How has this book changed your understanding of prayer and God's responses? What specific belief or practice will you change as a result?
- **Current Requests:** Review your current prayer requests. Are they aligned with God's will and glory, or are they primarily focused on your comfort and desires? What adjustments need to be made?
- **Past "No" Responses:** Think of three times you believed God said «No» to you. Can you now reinterpret those experiences through the lens of guidance, redirection, or preparation? What was God actually saying?
- **Living in the "Yes":** What practical steps will you take this week to position yourself to better hear and receive God's affirmative responses? Be specific.
- **Testimony Sharing:** Who needs to hear your story of God's faithfulness? How will you use your testimony of God's «Yes» to encourage someone else in their faith journey?

A Closing Prayer

Father God, thank You for revealing Your affirmative nature to us through Your Word and through the experiences of our lives.

Help us to trust You more deeply, seek You more earnestly, and align our hearts with Your will more completely.

When we face situations that seem like denials, give us wisdom to see Your redirection. When we're tempted to rush ahead of Your timing, grant us patience to wait for Your perfect plan. When our motives become self-centered, convict us by Your Holy Spirit and draw us back to seeking Your glory above all else.

We declare that You are faithful, You are good, and Your "Yes" is at work in our lives right now. We choose to trust You, follow You, and give You glory in all things.

In Jesus' mighty name, Amen.

Moment of Reflection

Before you close this book, take a moment to write down:

1. One new understanding of God's character you've gained.
2. One prayer request you'll commit to align with God's will.
3. One testimony of God's "Yes" you'll share with someone else this week.

May God bless you richly as you walk in the reality of His affirmative love.

BONUS CHAPTER TWELVE

A Personal Testament to God's Yes: God Said "Yes," She Said "I Do"

Excerpt from "Our Journey to 25 Years of Marriage," *by Jacquetta Renae Glover*

I prayed for my wife one day. I was at church, and the altar call started. The altar call, or the call to discipleship in some churches, is a time after a sermon that allows the parishioners to reflect on the message and get their life in the right direction.

I was in "need" of a wife at the time and thought I had done everything I needed to do to ready myself. I went up to the front of the church where Elder Brown, a stern and serious associate of my pastor, Pastor William Rogers, stood waiting for me. He prayed for me and my wife. The reality was that I did not know who she was at that time. I am confident that he did not know who she was either. Nevertheless, he prayed, and I agreed to things such as, "Lord, guide her and protect her," and "Give me, in her, what I need and her in me," and so on.

This is important to know as we continue to share. If you are single, praying for your spouse without name and face is a level of faith that is continually tested. You can be distracted when you pray with an ulterior motive. There can be a lot of counterfeit solutions that will be presented.

This is to say that I had an idea of the type and description of what I wanted my spouse to look like; dark, petite, of course beautiful, shapely, smart, and speaks French. Yes, speaks French, and that was a personal reason. Nevertheless, I petitioned prayers like that up until that day at the altar. You can imagine the sifting I had to go through to determine which one was the answer to my selfish prayer. "This one?" "This one Lord?" was my question with such a specific criterion.

I started praying for a nameless, faceless mate. I knew that if I did as I was taught, to show God how much I love Him by studying His Word, praying, living His Word, and spreading His Word, that He would bring my mate to me to experience Him in the flesh. I was presented a few counterfeit solutions before He brought our paths together, but I got through them. Let me explain.

The Counterfeit Solutions

One instance was when I was in the car on my way to the airport with two church members, a husband and his wife. They were in the front seat; I was in the back seat. On the way, the wife began to pray in the Spirit and received a word for me.

Let me stop here to set this up properly. I was in Europe, on my way back to the United States for my grandfather's funeral. I would be returning after about three or four weeks.

The couple had a daughter who would be coming to live with them while I was gone. She would be there when I returned.

Okay, now that you know this information, the wife received a word from the Lord: "My son, be patient. He hears you. God says that you will find your wife when you return."

I thought to myself, "When I return, your daughter will be here." I did not know or understand the word. Did God mean when I get back to the United States or Europe? But I knew one thing: the prophetic word from God would manifest itself if it is the word of God.

I did not doubt anything the Lord said through the wife, but I did complicate the matter with my limited understanding of what was said and my selfish desires. I left at the beginning of February 1990 for a funeral and returned to Europe engaged. Yes, I was scheduled to get married that next August 1990 to another beautiful woman, "FeeCee." She did not fit my order, but nice.

Needless to say, that did not work out, and I did check out the church members' daughter too. She was fine, for real, but she was not going to be good for me, and I will just say that and leave that alone.

Another counterfeit was when I was infatuated with a deacon's niece who was visiting from the States. He quickly let me know, "She ain't it!" What this deacon said to me next shook and changed my world, something that made me really think. I believe that God gave him the wisdom word for me. He said, "Do you think that you want to be married so much, so bad, that you lust over the thought of marriage?" He continued, "So much so, that you can't hear or even see what God is doing to bring you and your future wife together for that meet? Wait on the Lord, and He will direct your path. Pray for your wife now; for protection, guidance, and strength."

Wow, that was powerful! It hit me like a ton of bricks. I was even a little embarrassed that he had to tell me to get a grip. I prayed, "Lord, could I be so eager to get married that my judgment is clouded?" I told Him right then that I would not pay attention to another woman until my wife showed up (well, hey, I was desperate).

God began to reveal more about His plan for me. He said that I would go back to the U.S. and get married and bring my family back to Europe. He even told me who my pastor was going to be when I got back to Europe. What I didn't understand was when He said, "...and bring your family back to Europe." Be that as it may, I would have stood on His words to me and waited until He said, "This one!"

I worked hard waiting until September 16, 1990. After a crying conversation with God about His timeline, I pleaded that I couldn't go long or far without my wife. I was pleading for Him to bring her to me because I was not looking to mess things up anymore. I didn't want to be in a dead-end relationship because I knew that I was ready for full commitment. Now my wife will tell her side up to this point...

Her Side: The Meet Back Story

My life before meeting my husband was a whirlwind of relocations. After graduating, I moved from Alabama to Florida for school, then to Tennessee, then to the DC–Maryland–Virginia area multiple times, all before my 23rd birthday. As someone who loves roller coasters, this season of my life topped them all.

As most that know me, I love coaster rides. This part of my life topped all of them. I was at the church, and this handsome fella, okay, this fine "brutha" from the church, wooed me. He was light-skinned, hair just right, tall, a little muscle here and there, nice and looked good. He was funny and had business smarts. Making this short story shorter, we got married and lived in Alexandria.

I met my first husband in 1989. We dated, fell in love, and married that same year. I married him not knowing he was ill. Titus was nice, but I couldn't put my finger on the strange ways about him and the company he kept. He lost his battle to the Human Immune Deficiency Virus, better known as the AIDS virus. I was practically on the verge of a nervous breakdown. Even after finding that detrimental truth and discovering that he was bisexual, I cared for him until this 22-year-old wife could not care for him anymore. We agreed to return to our own hometowns. He moved back to Roanoke, and I went back to Birmingham.

Weeks later, I received a phone call from his sister informing me that Titus had asked me to come to see him. We spoke on the phone, and the last thing he said to me was, "Will you forgive me?" and to "hang in there." I went to see him, but the morning I arrived, he passed before I got there. My parents drove up to the funeral, and the plan was to come back home to Birmingham. But the Lord spoke to me, instructing me to return to D.C. At the time, I had no idea why I would be going back to the D.C. area. I just trusted that the still, small voice was not my own.

I had a hard time convincing my dad that I was not returning home with them. I had no place to live, no job, no car; just the word from the Lord. I called my old boss and informed her of my loss, and she offered me my job back and a place to stay. The Lord had already started opening doors for me. I received my husband's car, and my life appeared to balance. But after a week back in the city, I had a car accident and found there was no insurance on the car. There had been many sleepless nights, and it just seemed as if my whole world was crumbling around me. The Lord had a plan for me. I considered moving back home, but the Lord just kept saying, *stay.*

Gaytan was a career military man, and he was stationed in Germany at the time I was going through all my problems and situations. My husband was in Germany praying for his wife (that's me). No, he didn't know my name or my location, just that the Lord told him I was going through something, and his prayers would keep me. Daily he was praying for my health and strength, my mental state, not even knowing what I was going through.

He was getting ready to change duty stations, but he really loved Germany, so he was telling all of his friends that he was going to the mainland to get his family, and he would be back. People would say, "I didn't know you had a family back home," and he just said, "I don't yet, but I will."

He came to the church that Sunday, and later that evening, after the service, he introduced himself to me and gave me his number. I was not interested at the time. If you remember at the beginning of my story, I was telling about my first husband's passing. Well, this is just one month since his passing that we met. I took his number but did not call him and really didn't even have any intention of calling.

My girlfriend talked me into calling him after three days, and I called. We talked for a little while and decided we would see each other at Bible study that night. We talked briefly after service was over, and he wanted to take me out for dinner, but I told him about the accident I had earlier and that the next morning I was to go to court. He got so excited when I said that, and he just lit up like a light bulb. He said, "Can I go with you? That's what I do. I'm in law enforcement." I was glad he said that because I didn't know what to expect, being I had never stepped one foot inside a courtroom before. I told him, "Sure," I would be grateful if he came with me.

The next morning, he actually beat me to the courthouse. We had the hearing, and it was over pretty fast, so after, he asked me out for lunch. We drove back to his brother's house, where he was staying, for me to meet his brother and sister-in-law. On the way back to my car, he looked over at me and asked me, "What would you say if I told you I loved you?" I looked back at him and said, "I would say you're crazy. You don't even know me." We stopped for some ice cream and went to the park. Almost back to my car, he said the same thing again, but this time he had a serious look about himself.

I told him, "Look, there are some things about me you should know." I told him that I used to be married, and as a matter of fact, my husband had just died a month before, and that he died of AIDS, and I didn't know if I had it or would even get it, but I didn't want to be responsible for anyone else getting sick."

Gaytan looked at me and smiled. He said, "I already knew that about you." Someone he had asked that Sunday about me had already told him briefly about my situation. He went on to say that at the time I was going through the passing of my husband and my near breakdown, he had been praying for me. I was speechless at that point. We spent every available moment together; after work, on the weekends, wherever there was a free minute, we were together.

Well, in October, Gaytan proposed to me. At first, I was scared of what people would say or even think, but he was pretty sure that I was to be his wife. He told me of how he had put his request in with the Lord as to how he wanted his wife to look and what qualities and personality he was looking for, and I was it. Weird, huh? I thought so too. He told me that if we knew we were predestined to be together, why should we wait to please other people?

We drove to my hometown of Birmingham on a 36-hour road trip; twelve hours there, twelve hours to talk and meet my parents and talk to my pastor, Bishop O.L. Meadows, and a 12-hour drive back. He even asked my dad for my hand in marriage. After a long talk sitting at the kitchen table, Gaytan had expressed to my parents his love for me. While we were returning to D.C., we started planning a wedding. We made plans for a spring wedding (May, to be exact).

Well, December rolled around, and so did Desert Storm, and Gaytan's unit was being deployed. He was told that he would not be able to leave to go get married and that there was a great possibility that he would be deployed soon. Since my parents were in Alabama and his were in Kansas, he didn't want to take any chance that he would be sent away and not be married. We went to the courthouse and got married. Well, the Lord blessed, and he ended up working at a secure site on the other side of the military post and did not go to combat that time.

As a wedding present, our first child was conceived. There was not going to be a wedding any time soon. Two years went by, and we had our second child; the next year, our third; and the next year, our fourth. We just decided not to have a wedding, but I was granted a second chance at life and love, and I am so grateful and happy about it.

His Side: The Meet Back Story

Back to September 16, 1990. It was Sunday morning, and I wanted to go to church. I was a faithful member of "the Church," meaning the Church of God in Christ. I looked in the phonebook, a book widely used to find businesses and people back in the 80's and early 90's. (I cannot believe I am explaining this for younger readers.) I found the church in Maryland that I was drawn to.

I attended the morning service, and the pastor invited me to stay for dinner at the church. I was eating with one of the deacons of the church, and that's when it happened. This American beauty walked into my life. This one was like no other. I asked the deacon beside me what her name was. He said, "That's Renae. I think she is widowed." I said, "Really!" He replied that her husband had just died. I immediately went to God and said that I wouldn't let another woman derail me, and I just looked a little and moved on.

I was like a piece of raw meat in that church. I was getting a lot of attention; "fresh meat!" came to mind when I think about that day. I stayed for the evening service, and I was asked to speak. After service, I was assisting that deacon, I can't recall his name, with putting some items in his car. I brought her name up again, and he suggested that I introduce myself to her."

I told him that the only way I would talk to that "sista" is if she came to me. I was not falling for the trap. Then he closed the trunk of his car, and she was walking right by the car. I told him that was good enough for me, and I went for it. "Hello, my name is Gaytan." She replied that her name was Jacquetta.

Now she told her side up until this point. One thing I don't think she is sure about is the fact that she said, "I wasn't studdin' him." I know my "mackin'" and my game was on point, so...!

Me: About Her

I said that I met Renae in September 1990. I always tell people that our first date was when I went to court with Babe and bailed her out of jail. The truth is that she had to go to court for a traffic accident, and I offered to go with her for support. She had to pay a fine, and we went out to eat lunch.

I asked so many questions, as if I was going to marry her yesterday, that it didn't take long before she felt she had to tell me:

Babe: «I gotta tell you something before we move forward.» (She paused) "I was married, but my husband just died."

Me: «I know,» I replied.

Babe: «But he died of AIDS.»

Me: «I know,» I responded.

Babe: «Who told you?»

Me: "Curtis."

Let's pause to tell you who Curtis is. He was a friend I had just met at church. We were both ministers, and he knew that I was interested in Babe but wanted me to know her situation. Some readers might think he should have said nothing, but as you will find out, he actually showed his friendship. He didn't tell me not to talk to her or to beware. He just told me the story from what he knew.

He carefully informed me that she was married to this guy, and he had AIDS and died. But the interesting part was that he informed me that the "Mothers" of the church knew about his disease but didn't want to get involved because of what she might say to them. All hell broke loose in my head. *What the...?* They didn't warn her? They let her be deceived by a man that just wanted to be married before he died? Do you know what #%^# means? Well, I didn't say any of those words, but thoughts did cross my mind.

Had they told her, she could have at the very least confronted him with the matter and maybe been able to make her own informed decision about marrying him. *(We should be unapologetically saved. You can read more in the next book.)*

Anyway, she had to pay the court cost, and after she got out of court, we went on our first lunch date. We ate in Alexandria, and I took her back to my brother's house where we had dinner.

Somewhere in there, I asked her, "If I asked you to marry me, what would you say?" She replied, "Ask and find out." Well, I knew that I had to ask her father first, and we drove to Birmingham, Alabama, about two weeks later. I met her father, Hosea Nixon, and asked him if I could marry his youngest daughter.

He said yes, but I had already given her a ring beforehand to put some "skin in the game." I was serious when we drove twelve hours to Birmingham, stayed twelve hours, and drove back twelve hours. When I got back, I went straight to work; that's how serious I was about Jacquetta being my wife.

Babe: Ready to Follow

He told me that we would be going to Germany. I was excited and asked, "When?" He replied, "I don't know yet." He told me what the Lord had told him, so I believed it too. He told me our pastor would be Pastor Gordon. He had the whole plan for our next few years, family and all...

Me: Shaken but Not Stirred Up

The year 1992 brought a pivotal moment, time for my military re-enlistment. My commanding officer pulled me aside with what she considered sobering news: "If you re-enlist, there's a good chance you'll be PCSing (Permanently Changing Stations) to Korea. That's where everyone's orders are taking them these days."

Without hesitation, I responded with quiet confidence, "No ma'am, I'm scheduled to return to Germany."

Her expression shifted to one of polite bewilderment. "Do you have orders or some kind of documentation I'm not aware of?"

With crystal clarity, I explained, "The Lord told me when I arrived here that I was coming to get my wife and family, and then we would return to Germany together."

I could see the skeptical look across her face, the kind that was saying, "Sure thing, young Jedi" (a *Star Wars* line). Her doubt was understandable; Korea Command was actively reinforcing their forces, and every service member seemed destined for that assignment.

But they would have to execute that mission without me.

On re-enlistment day, standing before the entire company formation, something remarkable happened. As my commander handed me my official orders, she shared my bold declaration with everyone present; how I had confidently stated my destination despite all evidence pointing elsewhere. Then she announced my assignment: Germany.

Let me tell you something, brothers and sisters: when you align yourself with God's will for your life, you can take what He says to the bank. Believe it with unwavering confidence, knowing that He will direct your steps and provide everything necessary for your divine commission. You may be shaken by circumstances that seem to contradict His promises, but don't let yourself get stirred up into doubt and anxiety. He's got you covered.

Upon arriving in Germany, we immediately sought out a church home. However, the pastor wasn't the man the Lord had previously revealed to me. Instead of fretting or questioning God's word, I simply waited with expectant faith.

A few months later, I encountered that specific pastor at a conference. When I approached him and shared what the Lord had told me, he smiled with an expression that seemed to say, "Oh, young Padawan" (another *Star Wars* line), and gently informed me that he wasn't currently pastoring anywhere.

But I didn't retreat from what God had spoken. At that moment, I understood I was simply the messenger, delivering a word that would manifest in His perfect timing.

Fast-forward one year, and behold, the miraculous unfolded exactly as God had promised! This same pastor moved to our city to become the spiritual leader of our church. During his installation, he testified before the entire congregation about our conversation a year earlier, confirming the prophetic word the Lord had given me.

This experience reinforced a fundamental truth: you must believe that He is, and that He will fulfill every promise He makes. When God speaks, He doesn't lie, change His mind, or fail to follow through. His timeline may not match our expectations, but His faithfulness is absolutely certain.

The incredible love story we've shared here is just the beginning. Our complete journey, filled with even more miraculous confirmations of God's "Yes," will be revealed in our upcoming book. We invite you to watch for it, as it contains testimonies that will strengthen your faith in God's perfect orchestration of every detail of our lives.

Stay tuned for the rest of our amazing testimony of God's faithfulness in marriage, ministry, and life.

COMPLETE LIST OF BIBLE SCRIPTURES REFERENCED IN THIS BOOK

Genesis

- Genesis 1:1–2 (Creation)
- Genesis 6:6 (God grieves)
- Genesis 12:1–3 (Abraham's call)

Exodus

- Exodus 17:1–7 (Water from the rock: first instance)

Numbers

- Numbers 20:7–13 (Moses strikes the rock)
- 1 Samuel
- 1 Samuel 8:4–22 (Israel demands a king)
- 1 Kings
- 1 Kings 12 (Rehoboam's poor decision)

1 Chronicles

- 1 Chronicles 28:2–3 (David and the temple)
- Job
- Job 38–41 (God's response to Job)

Psalms

- Psalm 9:8 (God judges with equity)
- Psalm 23 (The Lord is my shepherd)
- Psalm 37:4 (Delight in the Lord)
- Psalm 51:1–12 (David's prayer for a clean heart)
- Psalm 139:23–24 (Search me, O God)

Proverbs

- Proverbs 3:5–6 (Trust in the Lord)
- Proverbs 6:16–19 (Things God hates)
- Proverbs 18:22 (Finding a wife)

Isaiah

- Isaiah 1:2 (Children who have rebelled)
- Isaiah 9:6–7 (Unto us a child is born)
- Isaiah 50:4 (The learned tongue)

Jeremiah

- Jeremiah 29:11 (Plans to prosper you)

Ezekiel

- Ezekiel 33 (The watchman)

Daniel

- Daniel 2–3 (Shadrach, Meshach, and Abednego)

Micah

- Micah 5:2 (Born in Bethlehem)

Malachi

- Malachi 3:10 (Bring the whole tithe)

Matthew

- Matthew 6:9–13 (The Lord's Prayer)
- Matthew 6:33 (Seek first the kingdom)
- Matthew 20 (Christ's death)
- Matthew 25 (Judgment of the nations)
- Matthew 26:39 (Not my will, but Yours)
- Matthew 28:18 (All authority given to Jesus)

Luke

- Luke 1 (Throne of David)
- Luke 1:34–35 (Virgin birth)
- Luke 2:1–7 (Jesus' birth in Bethlehem)

John

- John 3:16 (God so loved the world)
- John 4:24 (God is spirit)
- John 11 (I am the resurrection)
- John 14:6 (I am the way)
- John 14:9–14 (Greater works)
- John 16:24 (Ask in My name)
- John 19 (Jesus' death)
- John 20 (Resurrection appearances)

Acts

- Acts 1 (Ascension)
- Acts 2:41, 47 (Added to the Church)
- Acts 4:12 (No other name)
- Acts 5:29 (Obey God rather than men)

- Acts 7–9 (Stephen and Paul)
- Acts 16:30–31 (Believe in the Lord Jesus)

Romans

- Romans 1:16, 20 (The gospel is God's power; creation reveals God)
- Romans 3:23 (All have sinned)
- Romans 5:6–8 (Christ died for us)
- Romans 6:23 (Wages of sin)
- Romans 8:28 (All things work together for good)
- Romans 10:1, 4, 9–10 (Confess and believe)
- Romans 11 (Israel's salvation)
- Romans 12:2 (Transformed by renewing of mind)

1 Corinthians

- 1 Corinthians 4:2 (Faithful stewards)
- 1 Corinthians 6:19–20 (Your body is a temple)
- 1 Corinthians 15:3–4 (Gospel message)

2 Corinthians

- 2 Corinthians 1:18–20 (All promises are Yes and Amen)
- 2 Corinthians 5 (New creation; God made Him sin)
- 2 Corinthians 5:17, 21 (New creation; made sin for us)
- 2 Corinthians 12:7–9 (Paul's thorn in the flesh)

Galatians

- Galatians 4:7 (Sons and heirs)

Ephesians

- Ephesians 2:8–9 (Saved by grace through faith)
- Ephesians 3:20 (Able to do exceedingly abundantly)

Philippians

- Philippians 4:6 (Be anxious for nothing)

1 Thessalonians

- 1 Thessalonians 1:9 (Living and true God)
- 1 Thessalonians 4 (The Lord's coming)

2 Timothy

- 2 Timothy 2:15 (Rightly dividing the Word)

Hebrews

- Hebrews 4:14–16 (Come boldly to the throne)
- Hebrews 9:24, 26, 28 (Christ appeared to save)
- Hebrews 10 (Jesus at right hand of God)
- Hebrews 10:25 (Not forsaking the assembly)
- Hebrews 11:5–6 (Without faith impossible to please God)
- Hebrews 12:11 (Discipline produces righteousness)
- Hebrews 12:29 (Consuming fire)

James

- James 4:3, 17 (Ask with wrong motives; passive rebellion)

1 Peter

- 1 Peter 1:18–19 (Redeemed with precious blood)
- 1 Peter 2:22 (He did not sin)

- 1 Peter 3:18 (Christ suffered for sins)
- 1 Peter 5:7 (Cast your cares on Him)

1 John

- 1 John 1:5, 9 (God is light; confess sins)
- 1 John 3:2, 4, 5 (We shall be like Him; sin is lawlessness)
- 1 John 4:8–16 (God is love)
- 1 John 5:10, 13, 17 (Testimony of God; assurance; all unrighteousness is sin)

Revelation

- Revelation 13:8 (Lamb slain from foundation)

REFERENCE

PhD Statistics Reference (Chapter 1): Cambridge Database. *What percentage of Black Americans hold doctorates?* Retrieved from https://cambridgedb.com/what-percentage-of-black-americans-hold-doctorates.html

Book Reference (Chapter 6): Arterburn, S., Stoeker, F., & Yorkey, M. (2019). *Every Man's Battle, Revised and Updated 20th Anniversary Edition: Winning the War on Sexual Temptation One Victory at a Time*. WaterBrook.

Bible Translation: *The Holy Bible: English Standard Version, Containing the Old and New Testaments*. (2001). Crossway.

Dictionary Reference: Gove, P. B., & Merriam-Webster, Inc. (2002). *Webster's Third New International Dictionary of the English Language, Unabridged*. Merriam-Webster.

To Obtain Free Study Guide:
gaytanglover.com/lead-collection

www.ingramcontent.com/pod-product-compliance
Lightning Source LLC
LaVergne TN
LVHW010921110826
845149LV00013B/2440

* 9 7 9 8 9 9 3 9 1 7 3 1 3 *